COMMUNITY
LAND TRUSTS
AND INFORMAL
SETTLEMENTS IN
THE GLOBAL SOUTH

A Common Ground Monograph

COMMUNITY LAND TRUSTS AND INFORMAL SETTLEMENTS IN THE GLOBAL SOUTH

John Emmeus Davis
Line Algoed
María E. Hernández-Torrales

EDITORS

TERRA NOSTRA PRESS
Madison, Wisconsin, USA

TERRA NOSTRA PRESS

Center for Community Land Trust Innovation
3146 Buena Vista Street
Madison, Wisconsin, USA 53704

Publisher's Cataloging-in-Publication Data

Names: Davis, John Emmeus, editor. | Algoed, Line, editor. | Hernández-Torrales, María E., editor.
Title: Community land trusts and informal settlements in the Global South /
John Emmeus Davis ; Line Algoed ; María E. Hernández-Torrales, editors.
Series: Common Ground Monographs
Description: Includes bibliographical references. | Madison, WI: Terra Nostra Press, 2021.
Identifiers: Library of Congress Control Number: 2021903862 |
ISBN: 978-1-7362759-1-7 (paperback) | ISBN: 978-1-7362759-2-4 (ebook)
Subjects: LCSH Land trusts. | Land tenure. | Land use. | Land use, Urban. | Nature conservation. |
Landscape protection. | Sustainable development. | Sustainable development—Developing countries.
Economic development—Environmental aspects. | City planning—Environmental aspects. |
Community development. | Urban ecology (Sociology) |
BISAC POLITICAL SCIENCE / Public Policy / City Planning & Urban Development | LAW / Housing
& Urban Development | BUSINESS & ECONOMICS / Development / Sustainable Development |
SOCIAL SCIENCE / Sociology / Urban
Classification: LCC KF736.L3 W49 2021 | DDC 333.2—dc23

CONTENTS

Figures   vii

The Growth of CLTs in the Global South: An Introduction   ix
John Emmeus Davis, Line Algoed, and María E. Hernández-Torrales

1. Examining Responses to Informality in the Global South:
A Framework for Community Land Trusts and Informal Settlements   1
Patricia Basile and Meagan M. Ehlenz

2. Seeding the CLT in Latin America and the Caribbean:
Origins, Achievements, and the Proof-of-Concept Example of
the Caño Martin Peña CLT   31
*Line Algoed, María E. Hernández-Torrales, Lyvia Rodriguez Del Valle,
and Karla Torres Sueiro*

3. Adapting Features of Puerto Rico's Caño Martín Peña CLT to
Address Land Insecurity in the Favelas of Rio de Janeiro, Brazil   53
*Tarcyla Fidalgo Ribeiro, Line Algoed, María E. Hernández-Torrales,
Lyvia Rodríguez Del Valle, Alejandro Cotté Morales,
and Theresa Williamson*

4. A Watershed Land Trust in Honduras: Profile of Fundación Eco
Verde Sostenible   79
Kirby White and Nola White

5.   Seeding the CLT in Africa: Lessons from the Early Efforts to
      Establish Community Land Trusts in Kenya   87
      Claire Simonneau and Ellen Bassett, with Emmanuel Midheme

6.   The Origins and Evolution of the CLT Model in South Asia   105
      Hannah Sholder and Arif Hasan

7.   Challenges for the New Kid on the Block—Collective Property   123
      Liz Alden Wily

      About the Contributors   133

FIGURES

0.1	The "Classic" CLT	xii
1.1	Comparison of Informality Policies and the Community Land Trust Model	11
1.2	Conceptual Framework for CLTs in Informal Settlements	14
2.1	Aerial view of the Caño Martín Peña, San Juan, Puerto Rico	35
2.2	Streets within the Caño's neighborhoods, San Juan, Puerto Rico	36
2.3	Community council election, San Juan, Puerto Rico	38
2.4	Resident signing a surface rights deed, Caño Martín Peña CLT	44
2.5	Neighborhood mural: "residents as creators of our own future"	49
3.1	Fogueteiro favela, Central Rio de Janeiro, Brazil	55
3.2	Morro da Providência, Rio de Janeiro, Brazil	57
3.3	Vidigal favela, Rio de Janeiro, Brazil	58
3.4	Asa Branca favela street life, Rio de Janeiro, Brazil	61
3.5	Caño Martín Peña delegation visiting the Barrinha favela, 2018	70
4.1	Honduras mountains	81
4.2	Water source for a mountain village, Honduras	83
4.3	FECOVESO board of directors, Honduras, 2019	85
5.1	Location of the informal settlement of Tanzania-Bondeni, Kenya	90
5.2	Dwellings and elementary school, Tanzania-Bondeni, Kenya	95
5.3	Multi-storey residential building, Tanzania-Bondeni, Kenya	96
6.1	Roof-top view of Geneva Camp, Bangladesh	115

The Growth of CLTs in the Global South

An Introduction

John Emmeus Davis, Line Algoed,
and María E. Hernández-Torrales

Fifty years after the appearance of the first community land trust (CLT) in the United States, CLTs have increased in number and spread far beyond their country of origin. Today, there are approximately 280 CLTs operating in U.S. cities, suburbs, islands, and towns. Over 300 CLTs are up and running in the United Kingdom. Others have been established in Australia, Belgium, Canada, and France. Interest has been rising in Germany, Ireland, Italy, the Netherlands, Portugal, Scotland, and Spain.

To date, the proliferation of community land trusts has occurred mostly in the Global North. But that is changing, due in part to the Caño Martín Peña CLT in San Juan, Puerto Rico. The success of this high-profile strategy for regularizing tenure and securing the homes of families residing in seven informal settlements, an initiative which simultaneously secured the right of residents to participate in the process of deciding the development of an area they have called home for many decades, has attracted the attention of people living in similar situations in Latin America and the Caribbean. Community activists working in informal settlements in Africa and South Asia have taken note of the CLT as well, exploring whether some version of this strategy might be used to promote security of tenure within their own communities.

Community land trusts have been noticed too by the United Nations. At the 2016 Conference on Housing and Sustainable Urban Development in Quito, Ecuador, community land trusts were included among the "policies, tools, mechanisms, and financing models" named in the UN's *New Urban Agenda* for promoting access to housing and making cities more inclusive. CLTs were touted as one of several "cooperative solutions" for addressing, in the *Agenda's* words, "the evolving needs of persons and communities, in order to improve the supply of housing, especially for low-income groups, prevent segregation, and [prevent] arbitrary forced evictions and displacements . . . with special attention to programmes for upgrading slums and informal settlements."[1]

CLTs do, in fact, have a programmatic focus on promoting and preserving access to housing for low-income groups. Most CLTs also pay special attention to addressing the needs of people at risk of being displaced, either because they are residing on lands for which they do not hold formal title or because they are being priced out of areas where land values and housing costs are rapidly rising. Informal settlements, in particular, have been deemed by the United Nations to represent the embodiment of exclusion. CLTs, on the contrary, provide a platform for inclusion and participation.

This puts CLTs at the intersection of two worldwide movements for social change. The first is an increasingly powerful housing rights movement that is surfacing in cities around the world, championing a "right to the city," rent control, community-led development, and housing that remains permanently affordable. The second is occurring in countries where people who are land-insecure are struggling to gain recognition, registration, and legal protection for collective property, acreage that is used under some form of informal landholding system. Depending on the country, such property is termed communal, collective, customary, native, indigenous, or community land.[2]

The potential contribution of community land trusts to this latter movement is the focus of the present volume. Millions of low-income people in Latin America, the Caribbean, Africa, and South Asia have long inhabited parcels of land—or have long used land-based resources like waterways, forests, pastures, and arable fields—without possessing a legally sanctioned, formally registered right to do so. They live in homes their families may have constructed, improved, and occupied over several generations, but they are perched on lots from which they may someday be evicted. They depend on watersheds, woodlands, or farmlands for their livelihood, but they are using resources from which they may someday be excluded. Displacement looms as an ever-present possibility.

Featured in the chapters that follow are five studies of CLTs being implemented or explored as a strategy for enhancing land tenure security in informal communities in Puerto Rico, Brazil, Honduras, Kenya, and South Asia. The opening chapter by Patricia Basile and Meagan Ehlenz and the closing chapter by Liz Alden Wily situate these country-specific cases within a larger context of informality in the Global South and collective property rights throughout the world. All of the chapters in the present monograph, except for the one authored by Basile and Ehlenz, are drawn from a collection of twenty-six original essays published by Terra Nostra Press in June 2020, entitled *On Common Ground: International Perspectives on the Community Land Trust.*

WHAT'S IN A NAME?

Community land trusts are not all alike. Among the hundreds of CLTs that already exist or are presently being planned, there are numerous variations in how these organizations are structured, how their lands are utilized, how development is done, and how the stewardship of housing is operationalized. What is called a "community land trust" can vary greatly from one country to another, even from one community to another within the same country.

The basic features of the modern-day CLT were originally outlined in a seminal book that appeared in 1972.[3] The design for what was called in this book a "new model of land tenure for America" was drawn mostly from New Communities Inc., a rural settlement founded two years earlier by African-American activists. They had sought to combine community ownership of land, individual ownership of multi-family and single-family housing, and the cooperative organization of agricultural production. The book's authors drew, too, on a number of historical precedents, including the collectively owned lands of indigenous peoples, the town commons of New England, the *moshav ovdim* of Israel, the *ejidos* of Mexico, the *Ujamaa Vijijini* of Tanzania, and the *Gramdan* villages of India.[4]

The model described in 1972 also bore a resemblance to the mixed-ownership scheme that Ebenezer Howard had proposed in 1898 for the Garden Cities of England.[5] The houses, stores, orchards, and factories in the new towns he wanted to establish on the outskirts of major cities would be privately owned by individuals, cooperatives, or for-profit businesses, but the underlying land would be owned forever by a nongovernmental organization, created expressly for that purpose. These scattered parcels of land, despite their removal from the speculative market, would be made available for planned development and productive use through long-term ground leases, executed between the nonprofit landowner and myriad individuals who owned buildings or operated enterprises on the leaseholds. Land was to be held and managed on behalf of *all* residents – rich and poor, present and future – enabling a community to direct its own development, to determine its own fate, and to capture for the common good a majority of the gains in land value that society as a whole had helped to create.

To the mixed-ownership model pioneered in England, India, and elsewhere, the visionaries who created New Communities, Inc.—and the reflective practitioners who followed in their wake—added organizational and operational features of their own, turning the model into something different, something new. Community-owned land remained the foundation on which a CLT was to be established, with a private, nonprofit corporation holding and managing scattered parcels of land for the benefit of residents of a particular locale, especially low-income families in need of housing. What got *added* were mechanisms for ensuring that the development done by a CLT would be guided by the community, as would the organization itself. This was not development from above, dictated by a governmental body, a charitable investor, or a benevolent provider of social housing. It was development from below, directed by residents of the community a CLT had been organized to serve. Ownership and empowerment went hand-in-hand.[6]

Added, too, was an operational commitment to the *stewardship* of any lands entrusted to the CLT and of any buildings erected on its lands, most of which would be owned

Fig. 0.1. The "Classic" CLT

COMMUNITY
(Organization)

LAND
(Ownership)

TRUST
(Operation)

by somebody else. Projects pursued by a CLT were designed to ensure that housing, nonresidential buildings, and other land uses would remain continuously affordable, long after development was done.[7]

These distinctive features of ownership, organization, and operation, overlapping and interacting in a dynamic model of place-based development, became known as the "classic" CLT. Almost as soon as nearly everyone came to agree on this particular conception and configuration of the community land trust, however, the model began to be modified in countless ways. Variations arose in every feature of the "classic" CLT, as practitioners in different places adapted it to fit conditions, needs, and priorities in their own communities or to fit customs and laws in their own countries.

This continuing process of innovation and adaptation has helped the CLT to spread across a disparate international landscape and to thrive in a range of settings. At the same time, the diversity of meanings attached to the model and the variety of ways in which CLTs are structured has introduced a degree of difficulty to the task of explaining exactly what a CLT might be. Today, there is ambiguity—even a dose of controversy—to be found in the description and implementation of every component.

Community. Throughout the world, most organizations that call themselves a CLT are committed to involving a place-based population in their activities, incorporating a participatory ethos into their organization's purposes, practices, and structure. People who live on the CLT's lands and those who live nearby are encouraged to become voting members of the organization. They are recruited to serve on its governing board.[8] They are invited to participate in shaping the uses and projects proposed by the CLT. Development is "community-led," along with the organization that initiates and oversees that development.

Ambiguity enters the picture because of the varying arrangements that CLTs employ in striving to engage and to empower their community. Controversy arises because some CLTs have dispensed with community altogether, causing critics to question whether they should even be considered a "real" CLT. The traditional model's distinctive features of ownership and operation might be present, but residents who are served by the program neither govern nor guide it; that is, "community" is missing from the organizational make-up of the entity doing development. Variations like these create perennial challenges for CLT advocates whenever they try to reach a consensus as to what deserves to be deemed a "community land trust."[9]

Land. The typical CLT is a nonprofit organization that removes land permanently from the marketplace, managing it on behalf of a place-based community while making it available for long-term use by individuals and organizations. Title to the buildings on a CLTs land, either those existing when the CLT acquired the land or those constructed later on, is held individually by any number of parties—homeowners, cooperatives, businesses, gardeners, farmers, etc. The underlying land is leased from the CLT by the buildings' owners.

This mixed-ownership arrangement blurs the legal and conceptual boundary between conventional categories of tenure, where real property is presumed to be one thing or the other. A community land trust messes up this tidy picture, for it is balanced half-way between the two extremes of *individual property*, owned and operated primarily for the purpose of promoting private interests; and *collective property*, owned and operated to promote a common interest. The CLT tilts toward the former in its treatment of buildings. It tilts toward the latter in its treatment of land, making the CLT a first cousin to cooperatives, co-housing, and various forms of communal, collective, and tribal land.

Although a CLT's lands are frequently and fairly characterized as "community-owned" or, in the parlance of the present series, as "common ground," these landholdings are neither collectively nor cooperatively owned by the people living on them or around them. Title is held exclusively by the CLT. A community land trust is ownership for the common good, not ownership in common.[10]

There are places, however, where the separation of ownership is made difficult (or impossible) by quirks in the property laws of a particular country or by the quibbles of prospective funders. CLTs have sometimes been compelled, therefore, to retain ownership of buildings as well as the land or to relinquish ownership of both, while imposing long-lasting restrictions on the use and affordability of these properties. Another variation has been developed in Puerto Rico, where the Caño Martín Peña CLT holds the underlying land but uses a durable surface rights deed, rather than a ground lease, to provide security of tenure for people who own and occupy houses on the CLT's land. Some of these residents are living on sites their families have inhabited for nearly a hundred years.

Trust. Although "trust" is part of their given name, CLTs have rarely been established as real estate trusts.[11] Most are NGOs—private, nonprofit corporations with a charitable purpose of meeting the needs of populations who are regularly underserved by both the market and the state. "Trust" refers not to how a CLT is organized, but to how it is operated. "Trust" is what a CLT *does* in overseeing the lands and buildings under its care and in performing the duties of stewardship. Foremost among these duties is the preservation of affordability, ensuring long-term access to land and housing for people of modest means and preventing their displacement due to gentrification and other pressures. Steward-ship also includes such responsibilities as preventing deferred maintenance in housing and other buildings on the CLT's land and intervening, if necessary, to protect occupants against predatory lending, arbitrary eviction, mortgage foreclosure, and other threats to security of tenure.

Some CLTs are focused less on the provision of housing, however, than on the preser-vation of watersheds, woodlands, or agricultural lands, either in rural or urban areas. The stewardship responsibilities of a CLT entrusted with managing such lands can look very different than the stewardship needed when affordable housing is a CLT's operational focus.

Model. The first book to describe the community land trust called it a "new model of land tenure." It has been regularly called a "model" ever since. A number of practitioners and researchers have grown uncomfortable with the term, however. Some object because "model," from their perspective, carries a negative connotation of something experimen-tal, unfinished, unreliable. They point to fifty years of success, saying that the CLT is no longer a working prototype, but a road-tested, high-performing vehicle that has gone the distance and proven its effectiveness under challenging conditions.

Others object because "model" seems to imply there is only one "proper" way of struc-turing a CLT, when the reality unfolding around the world is the emergence of many different structures and strategies. Each country and community is composing its own variation on the theme of CLT classic. "Model" tends to be especially problematic for organizers in the Global South, for whom the term is tainted with a whiff of Yankee ar-rogance, as if there exists some universal blueprint for building a CLT, indelibly stamped with "Made in America." Most organizers outside of the Global North tend to avoid the term, therefore, preferring to describe the CLT as a mechanism, instrument, or tool.

On the other hand, there are still many practitioners and researchers for whom "mod-el" remains their term of choice. It holds for them a positive, prescriptive message of a design, pattern, or practice that is exemplary and worthy of consideration by anyone in-volved with affordable housing or community development. They are unconcerned that "model" may also suggest that the CLT is still being fine-tuned, still in a state of flux. After all, a restless search for better ways of configuring and combining ownership, or-ganization, and operation is part of the reason that CLTs have been able to thrive in so many political and economic environments, some of which were initially hostile to their germination.

A few of the contributors to the present monograph have continued the custom of referring to the CLT as a "model," but we have not discouraged contributors who have preferred to call it something else. Even authors who regularly refer to the CLT as a "mod-el" also describe it, on occasion, as a strategy, platform, mechanism, vehicle, construct, or tool—sometimes within the same essay. These terms are used interchangeably throughout the monograph.

WHAT'S SHARED?

There is a lack of conceptual uniformity in the current collection of essays, when it comes to describing what a CLT is or does, but commonalities exist nonetheless. What unites CLT practitioners and scholars across the world is more important than what separates them. Woven throughout the monograph's chapters are recurring themes that provide something of a *lingua franca* for understanding what it means for an organization to be a CLT and to behave like one. There is a shared commitment to reinventing and repurposing real estate for the common good. There is a shared conviction that community-owned land, in particular, is likely to do a better job of promoting equitable and sustainable development than land that is commodified and owned individually, especially in informal settlements populated by groups that have long been disadvantaged and disempowered.

Another trait that is shared by most CLT scholars and practitioners is a conviction that the whole of a CLT is greater than the sum of its parts. Across the diverse landscape of CLTs, ownership, organization, and operation are not configured exactly the same in every settlement and country. Wherever this strategy has been adopted, however, there is a general recognition that it takes more than a single component to make a CLT; it takes more than the reinvention of any one of them to bend the arc of development toward a fairer distribution of property and power. Community-owned land, by itself, is not enough. Community-led development is not enough. Permanently affordable housing is not enough. It is their *combination* that gives a CLT its distinctive identity and transformative potential.[12]

To be sure, there are places in the world where CLTs have been effective without adopting every feature of the "classic" CLT. That model is no longer a template, but it remains a touchstone. It is where most people start, when striving to adapt this complex form of tenure to their own situations. It is where most people hope a CLT will lead, when envisioning a better outcome from their arduous, virtuous labors, whether providing affordable housing, rebuilding residential neighborhoods, regularizing tenure in informal settlements, or preserving productive lands, pristine watersheds, or local enterprises at risk of being lost to market pressures.

When land is owned for the common good of a place-based community, present and future; when development is done by an organization that is a creature of that community, rooted in it, accountable to it, and guided by it; when stewardship is deliberate, diligent, and durable . . . justice is more likely to be achieved. And more likely to last. That is the moral impetus and lofty promise of common ground.

Notes

1. United Nations. *New Urban Agenda.* Adopted at the Conference on Housing and Sustainable Urban Development (Habitat III) in Quito, Ecuador, on 20 October 2016 and endorsed by the United Nations General Assembly at its sixty-eighth plenary meeting of the seventy-first session on 23 December 2016. (Paragraph 107 appears on page 27.) Available at: *http://habitat3.org/the-new-urban-agenda/*.

2. These terms for socially-based, collective landholding are borrowed from Liz Alden Wily, "Challenges for the New Kid on the Block—Collective Property," Chapter 7 in the present volume.

3. Robert Swann, Shimon Gottschalk, Erick S. Hansch, and Edward Webster, *The Community Land Trust: A Guide to a New Model for Land Tenure in America* (International Independence Institute/Center for Community Economic Development, 1972).

4. Other intellectual influences and historical precedents acknowledged by the book's authors included Henry George, Ralph Borsodi, Mildrid Loomis, and the planned, leased-land communities of Bryn Gweled Homesteads near Philadelphia and Morningside Gardens outside of New York City.

5. Ebenezer Howard, *Garden Cities of Tomorrow* (Swan Sonnenshein & Co., 1902).

6. This interweaving of ownership and empowerment was never far from the minds of the African-Americans who pioneered the first CLT. A brochure for New Communities, Inc., printed in the 1970s, described the purpose of a land trust in this way: "It is people holding land together as a community; it is 'people power,' the security of holding and owning together the land which, through development and use, will bring them the power to stand on their own two feet."

7. This is achieved through the CLT's ownership of the underlying land and its imposition of contractual controls over the buildings' rents and resales. Aside from determining how the land is to be used, these contractual con-trols—typically imposed through a 99-year ground lease—regulate the occupancy, upkeep, improvement, financing, behest, and resale of any buildings sited on the CLT's land.

8. Organizationally, the model promoted by the Institute for Community Economics during the 1980s had an open membership and a three-part board, representing the interests of the people who live on the CLT's land, people who live within the CLT's service area, and institutions that served that geography, including government, churches, banks, businesses, and other NGOs. See Institute for Community Economics, The Community Land Trust Hand-book (Emmaus PA: Rodale Press, 1982).

9. To a certain degree, we have sidestepped this definitional debate in the present volume by featuring a number of organizations that self-identify as a community land trust, even

if they do not exhibit every feature of what is known in the USA as the "classic" CLT. Our ecumenical embrace had limits, however. We admitted to the com-pany of CLTs only organizations that were committed to removing land permanently from the stream of com-merce, placing it under the ownership or control of a designated community and stewarding that land for the common good.

10. This echoes the earliest description of the CLT: "The community land trust is not primarily concerned with common ownership. Rather, its concern is ownership for the common good, which may or may not be combined with common ownership." Swann et al (1972), op cit., page 1. Although the people living on a CLT's land do not hold title to the underlying land, the resale formula used by some CLTs does provide for a modest increase in the homeowner's equity if the land has appreciated in value during the home-owner's tenure.

11. Trusts are established by individuals to control the distribution of their property, either during the individuals' lifetimes or after their death. Property is often real estate, but it can also be stocks, bonds, or other income-generating assets. The person who creates the trust is called the "settlor." The person who holds the property for another's behalf is the "trustee." The latter takes title to the property (although, under a "revocable trust," the settlor may later reclaim ownership). Proceeds from the trust are distributed by the trustee to a specific list of beneficiaries named by the settlor when the trust was established.

12. The synergy that comes from combining the components of a CLT is explored in greater detail in John Emmeus Davis, "Better Together: The Challenging, Transformative Complexity of Community, Land, and Trust." Chapter 26 in J. Davis, L. Algoed and M. Hernández-Torrales (eds.), *On Common Ground: International Perspectives on the Com-munity Land Trust* (Madison WI: Terra Nostra Press, 2020).

1.

Examining Responses to Informality in the Global South
A Framework for Community Land Trusts and Informal Settlements[1]

Patricia Basile and Meagan M. Ehlenz

Abstract

Informality has been a predominant source of affordable housing for the urban poor in the Global South. Despite many efforts to eliminate and/or improve informal settlements, these communities still prevail as one of the only housing options for low-income households burdened by exclusion, dispossession, and stigma. This article evaluates the potential for and impediments to community land trusts (CLTs) as an alternative response to informality. We compare the CLT model to predominant policy responses to informality to understand its strengths and weaknesses. Based on this analysis, we propose a conceptual framework delineating the main conditions necessary to implement the CLT model within informal settlements in the Global South. This framework may inform the work of communities, governments, practitioners, and researchers pursuing an alternative response to housing informality. This study expands the existing understanding about CLTs and their possibilities for application in the Global South.

1. INTRODUCTION

In 2009, the Caño Martín Peña Community Land Trust (CMP-CLT) received ownership of 200 acres along the banks of the Martín Peña Channel in San Juan, Puerto Rico (World Habitat n.d.). This non-profit, community-based organization, sought to transition vulnerable informal settlements into safe, affordable housing alongside environmental remediation efforts. The formation of CMP-CLT represented one step in a contested journey to provide housing security and improve quality of life for thousands of families. The project embodies a limited instance of how the community land trust (CLT) model, which has primarily been applied within U.S. and European contexts, could be adapted to respond to housing informality and affordability concerns in the Global South.

This essay explores the possibilities for and impediments to the CLT model as a policy approach for informal communities in the Global South. Worldwide, one in eight people inhabit informal settlements (U.N. Habitat, 2016) and frequently lack property titles and basic infrastructure. Government and policy actors have pursued several strategies to address informal settlements. Although their efforts have alleviated some affordable housing pressures, they have not resolved the problem (Gilbert, 2001; McBride & French, 2011): close to one billion people remain in informal settlements, often burdened by social, economic, and spatial exclusion and stigma (Davis, 2006). Could CLTs offer a secure, community-empowered response?

We begin with a review of existing theories of urban informality, as well as three prevalent policy responses. Next, we discuss the origin, theory, and practice of CLTs and review two instances of CLTs in the Global South. Subsequently, we examine the potential for and impediments to CLTs as an informal settlement strategy relative to existing approaches. We also offer a conceptual framework for the application of CLTs in the Global South. We conclude with a discussion of the implications of the model for the Global South.

2. INFORMALITY DEBATES AND POLICIES

Informal settlements are self-produced communities, normally occupying land to which residents have no legal claim. Classified as informal due to their lack of compliance to codes, laws, and regulations, they are frequently viewed in stark terms: for instance, as unsanitary places with accumulated poverty (Davis, 2006) or as an alternate urban reality for the entrepreneurial poor (De Soto, 2000). Postcolonial scholarship has dismissed dichotomous characterizations, however. Rather than defining informality by its status outside the state, scholars interpret urban informality as a mode of urbanization (AlSayyad, 2004; Watson, 2009), thereby embracing a framework with patterns and norms that dictate urban transformation processes (Roy, 2005). For instance, state processes produce informality through decisions about where, when, and how to enforce regularization[2] laws – or not (Agamben, 1998). In this sense, informality represents a mode of governing, in which certain spaces and bodies are deemed illegal while others are allowed to thrive (da Silva Telles, 2010; Roy, 2005).

State-sponsored informality interventions are more than a matter of bureaucracy or technicality. They embody a complicated political struggle, embedded in the materialization and effectiveness of such policies (Roy, 2005). We review three predominant typologies of intervention—social housing, upgrading, and land titling, presenting their strengths, failures, and critiques.

2.1. Mass Social Housing

Mass social housing (MH)[3] is a century-old strategy (de Duren, 2018a), seeking to elim-inate informal housing through the construction of large-format, owner-occupied social (or public) housing (Burgess, 1978). MH advocates argue that homeownership advances household wealth (e.g., Rappaport, 2010; Retsinas & Belsky, 2004) and, consequently, economic development (Balchin, 2013). Other objectives include reducing housing sup-ply deficits, improving living conditions, and increasing social stability (Kowaltowski et al., 2015; Macedo, 2010).

The effects of MH projects are mixed (Kowaltowski et al., 2019). While they have contributed to improved quality of life, increased resident social status, and revitalized public spaces (e.g., da Costa & do Nascimento, 2016; Mastrodi & Zaccara, 2016; Rufino, 2016), MH projects have also failed residents because of peripheral siting, large develop-ment scales, repetition of monotonous designs, and lack of consideration for users' needs and wants (Buckley, Kallergis, & Wainer, 2016; Kowaltowski et al., 2019; Peek, Hordijk, & d'Auria, 2018). The peripheral location of urban MH projects tends to be isolated, inciting social segregation and presenting challenges of urban mobility and affordability (Acolin & Green, 2017; Moura, 2014; Ukoje & Kanu, 2014). Further, MH projects fre-quently value unit quantity over construction quality (de Duren, 2018a; Gilbert, 2014). These shortfalls can put additional financial pressure on residents, including increased maintenance costs, taxes, and service fees. These burdens call into question the benefits (or hidden costs) for households relocated from informal settlements into poor-quality MH. Lastly, while MH projects target low-income households, they often exclude vul-nerable populations without verifiable income (e.g., informal workers, migrants, and informal settlement residents) (de Duren, 2018b; Rolnik, 2013a). This highlights a sub-stantial gap in the housing need. There are also conflicts about MH objectives, which often emphasize economic growth and job creation over the provision of affordable housing (Rolnik, 2013a; Valença & Bonates, 2010). The privatization of social housing can further exacerbate these challenges (Rolnik, 2013a, 2013b). Collectively, scholars argue MH models expose chasms between creating affordable housing units and address-ing the realities of urban informality in the Global South.

2.2. Upgrading

Upgrading models involve the provision of basic infrastructure and amenities (e.g., play-grounds, public plazas), focused on improving the physical environment of informal set-tlements. Self-help scholars initially inspired this strategy. They recognized the capacity of low-income households to build their homes as resources become available (Abrams, 1966; Mangin, 1967; Turner, 1968, 1972); thus, self-help advocates argued governments and other non-profit organizations should spend their resources on basic infrastructure provision (van Lindert, 2016). Upgrading is usually a top-down initiative, but many upgrading programs have incorporated participatory efforts in their decision-making processes (Imparato & Ruster, 2003; Sholder & Hasan, 2020). Not only is upgrading less expensive than relocating residents to urban peripheries (Gulyani & Bassett, 2007), but it may also preserve existing social ties (Mangin, 1967).

Several studies highlight the positive impacts of upgrading projects (Atuesta & Soares, 2018; Gilbert, 2003; Keare & Parris, 1982; Lee-Smith & Memon, 1988). Upgrading programs can deliver community health benefits, including improved mental health and reduction of communicable diseases (Butala, VanRooyen, & Patel, 2010; Shortt, & Hammett, 2013; Turley et al., 2013), although the durability of health benefits is contested (Marais, & Ntema, 2013; Minnery et al., 2013; Werlin, 1999). Infrastructure investments can enhance de facto and perceived tenure security within settlements, instilling residents with a greater sense of permanence even in the absence of legal land titles (De Souza, 2001; Gilbert, 1990, 2002; Hylton, & Charles, 2018; Kiddle, 2010), increasing resident willingness to invest in their own homes (Handzic, 2010).

Many upgrading results are mixed. Since the 1990s, upgrading projects have embraced participatory decision-making processes with some benefits (Kiefer & Ranganathan, 2018; Mensah et al., 2017); others contest these benefits, citing constraints on resident empowerment (Berriane, 2010; De Geest & De Nys-Ketels, 2019; McFarlane, 2008). Similarly, scholars express concerns about infrastructure standards, as well as sufficient cost-recovery on investments (Atuesta & Soares, 2018; Gulyani & Bassett, 2007). And, much like MH projects, there are concerns about who benefits (Bredenoord & van Lindert, 2010; Verma, 2000): Upgrading may result in changes to social structures within informal settlements, potentially contributing to gentrification and displacement of tenants and highly vulnerable residents (Comelli, Anguelovski, & Chu, 2018; Davis, 2006).

Major criticisms also emphasize the prioritization of physical redevelopment over livelihoods, wages and political capacity in upgrading efforts, characterized by Roy (2004) as the *aestheticization of poverty*. While the literature suggests that upgrading models can effectively improve physical development, living standards, health, and de facto security of tenure, the model appears less equipped to address social and economic challenges for existing residents, nor do most projects offer strong examples of resident participation and empowerment.

2.3. Individual Land Titling

Individual land titling seeks to regularize informal settlements through the provision of legal titles to parcels of land on which people already live and on which, in many cases, they have built permanent or semi-permanent housing (Deinlnger & Binswanger, 1999; Payne, Durand-Lasserve, & Rakodi, 2009). The policy took hold during the 1990s and early 2000s, partially in response to De Soto's *The Mystery of Capital* (2000). De Soto contends titling is key to reducing informal settlement poverty and is claimed to be more cost-effective than other approaches (Gilbert, 2002; McAuslan, 1985). The model can also expand local tax bases through title acquisition (Cohen, 2001; Sanyal, 1996).

While some claim that individual land titling ensures access to formalized markets (Panaritis, 2007), housing investments, and other social benefits (Galiani & Schargrodsky, 2010), the model's results are contested. A broad discourse disputes De Soto's claims about the effectiveness of individual land titling in reducing poverty in informal settlements (e.g., Gilbert, 2012; Payne, Durand-Lasserve, & Rakodi, 2009). Although individual titling can improve tenure security, it does not significantly reduce poverty (Payne, Durand-Lasserve, & Rakodi, 2009). Scholarship in Colombia, Peru and Brazil has not found associations between titling and improved housing markets, employment opportunities, safety, or access to formal credit (Gilbert, 2002; Kagawa & Turkstra, 2002; Perlman, 2016).

Research also reveals several negative impacts of individual land titling. Titles can reinforce gender hierarchies and divisions, supporting vulnerable social constructs for women (Roy, 2003). They can generate unexpected financial burdens for residents, such as property taxes (Ward, 1989), spurring involuntary home sales (Johnson Jr, 1987; Peattie, 1982). Further, individual titling is often not appropriate for extremely low-income households who cannot absorb the additional financial obligations attached to property deeds (Payne, Durand-Lasserve, & Rakodi, 2009; Shirgaokar, & Rumbach, 2018). Other secondary impacts of individual titling include rising rents and potential displacement of tenants due to rising costs of living associated with mandatory taxes and services, and increase in the value of land in the community (Johnson Jr, 1987; Payne, 2001; Peattie, 1982). Some worry that individual titles transform homes into marketable commodities, causing market shifts that induce gentrification and displacement of owners, although evidence is limited (Silva & Mautner, 2016; Varley, 2002) and unconvincing (e.g., Durand-Lasserve, 2006). There is one exception. Evidence suggests that individual land titling can make informal settlements in prime locations (e.g., adjacent to wealthy neighbourhoods or scenic views) more valuable, providing opportunities for outside investors to monetize tenure regularization for profit (Varley, 2017). This process makes low-income residents of such prime locations more vulnerable to displacement.

Others contend individual titling does not address informal settlement needs, as basic infrastructure and tenure security do not require legal titles (Aristizabal & Gomez, 2002; Fernandes & Varley, 1998; Hylton & Charles, 2018; Varley, 1987). Even without formal ownership safeguards, many households in informal settlements feel sufficiently secure to invest in their domiciles (Briggs 2011; De Souza, 2001; Durand-Lasserve, 2006; Gulyani & Bassett, 2007). De facto tenure security is based on control of the dwelling unit and underlying land, independent of who holds the title to the building and/or the land. Several aspects can influence de facto security of tenure, such as the time length of occupation of the settlement, the size of the settlement, existence of infrastructure, cohesion of the community as well as third-party support and political acceptance (Van Gelder, 2010). This de facto tenure security can render titling largely irrelevant, effectively shielding residents from eviction and displacement (Kironde, 2006; Sims, 2002). Combined with a lack of evidence for poverty reduction, individual land titling alone cannot sufficiently resolve the issues of housing quality, quantity, and affordability that plague informal settlements in the Global South (Varley, 2017).

3. REVIEW OF THE CLT MODEL

Existing informality policies reveal substantial gaps related to community empowerment, wealth-building, quality of life, and long-term security. Thus, we examine another affordable housing strategy that emphasizes these features.

Property ownership is often considered binary: one owns or rents a home. There is, however, a third option that defines ownership not as a monolith, but a bundle of entitlements that can be distributed among multiple parties (Institute for Community Economics, 1982). In traditional freehold ownership, a property owner retains full title to both land and improvements; leasehold ownership typically divides property rights among two parties (e.g., a landowner and tenant) (Ehlenz, 2014). By contrast, CLT models grant rights to structural improvements to a homeowner and land title to a non-profit steward acting on behalf of a place-based community (Davis, 2010b).

Two principles guide CLT models: (1) permanent affordability of the building, achieved through limits on resale appreciation; and (2) stewardship of the property, both the building and the land, by a non-profit corporation and its community-represented board (Ehlenz & Taylor, 2019). CLTs are a prominent form of shared equity homeownership, characterized by three components (Davis, 2010b, 9): (1) A non-profit organization owns the land and maintains open membership; (2) the membership elects the majority of the organization's governing board; and (3) the governing board is "tripartite," with equal representation from CLT residents, non-CLT community members, and "public interest" representatives. CLTs exists alongside, but apart from, conventional housing markets, prioritizing the preservation of affordable housing subsidies through limits on resale equity and community-led ownership of the underlying land.

CLTs originated in 1960s in the rural U.S., where they emphasized affordable, secure housing, as well as farming and food cooperatives (Ehlenz & Taylor, 2019). The CLT model has since expanded: in 2017, the National Community Land Trust Network included more than 300 U.S. CLTs within its membership (National Community Land Trust Network, n.d.). CLTs have also expanded within the Global North, illustrated by a variety of start-ups and applications of the model within the United Kingdom, European countries, and Australia (e.g., Aernouts & Ryckewaert, 2018; Bunce, 2016; Cabré & Andrés, 2018; Crabtree, 2006; Lang & Stoeger, 2018; Mullins & Moore, 2018).

Research highlights several strengths of CLTs, including affordable housing provision, successes for households and communities, wealth-building for low-income CLT home-owners—achieved through lower purchase prices (Davis, 2017) – and affordable loan access (Theodos, et al., 2017). CLT homeowners earn more on their housing investment than if they had invested a comparable amount in stocks or bonds (e.g., Davis, 2017; Temkin, Theodos, & Price, 2010). CLTs also perform well in comparison to conventional homeownership strategies: CLT owners had lower foreclosure rates relative to non-CLT owners (Thaden, 2011); affordable subsidies were preserved over time (Jacobus & Davis, 2010); and CLT homes offered stability for owners (Temkin, Theodos, & Price, 2013).

CLTs also provide a range of less tangible benefits. Recent studies highlight the model's contributions to resident perceptions of security, stability, and improved quality of life (e.g., Martin et al., 2019; Thaden, Greer, & Saegert, 2013;). As a steward, the CLT organization lends credibility to the model, supporting residents with ongoing assistance (e.g., home maintenance or resale support) and minimizing financial risks (e.g., predatory loans, foreclosure) (e.g., Davis, 2017; Ehlenz, 2018; Thaden & Rosenberg, 2010).

Yet, the CLT model does face challenges. By definition, CLTs require a long-lasting, well-staffed non-profit to retain land ownership, facilitate home sales, protect affordability, and foster sustained community involvement. These types of organizations can be difficult to develop from scratch, absent an existing community institution (e.g., Ehlenz, 2018). Securing land and financial resources is also challenging, constraining the CLT's reach and threatening its long-term viability (Theodos et al., 2017).

CLTs can face technical and perceptual barriers as well, since they eschew conventional housing markets, retaining subsidies across transactions and limiting resale equity. This requires CLTs to pursue education, outreach, and buy-in for local governments, financial actors, and potential homeowners (Davis, 2010a; Theodos et al., 2017). CLTs may require modifications to existing regulations in order to function within a local housing market (Davis, 2017; Zonta, 2016).

Last, recent scholarship has demonstrated a number of CLTs in the US drifting away from their founding purposes and structures. Conceptually, the model emphasizes the role of *community*, including collective governance and empowerment. However, the model's implementation and adaptation in a number of cities has increasingly been called into question (DeFilippis, Stromberg, & Williams, 2018; Vuong, 2016). As CLTs have expanded their affordable housing roles, some argue they have sublimated their historic commitment to community governance and control.

3.1. CLTs in the Global South?

CLT potential and adoption have increased over recent decades. However, its reach remains limited, with small shares of housing in the U.S. and other Global North countries. There have been relatively few conversations about the CLT's potential within the Global South. Yet, parallels between CLT principles and Global South housing conventions offer an opportunity. For instance, the questionable relationship between individual property titling and tenure security embodies a central debate for informal housing; the CLT model offers a different approach that may offer more secure housing, alongside community-protected land tenure. Similarly, incremental housing practices—the gradual expansion of a unit as a household acquires resources—is common in the Global South; this concept is compatible with the CLT's participatory and community empowerment aims.

The literature offers two primary case studies of Global South-based CLTs: the Tanzania-Bondeni CLT in Kenya and the Caño Martín Peña CLT in Puerto Rico. Both cases offer insights for the potential of CLTs in informal settlements. This section briefly reviews the context, implementation, and results of each case.

3.1.1. The Tanzania-Bondeni CLT: Voi, Kenya

In the 1990s, the Tanzania-Bondeni (TB) informal settlement in Voi, Kenya experienced upgrading, with an emphasis on securing collective land rights and preserving resident benefits (Bassett, 2005). The CLT model offered a community-led approach that could retain upgrading benefits for residents, support community control, and limit market-based consequences, including absentee ownership and land sales (Bassett, 2005). The project included infrastructure investments, improved housing, and housing financing, as well as planning and technical support.

TB residents selected the CLT model from three options—individual titles, a CLT, or a housing co-operative (Yahya, 2002). The model required significant modifications to Kenyan law and administrative frameworks (Bassett, 2005, 2007). In the U.S., the CLT organization serves as the landholder and community steward; Kenyan law restricts ownership (Syagga, 2006). To hold land in perpetuity, Tanzania-Bondeni CLT (TB-CLT) needed to establish both a legal entity to manage the CLT and a separate trust to retain the land title (Midheme & Moulaert, 2013).

Bassett and Jacobs (1997) identified several critical factors for TB-CLT's development and execution. Key among them was the community's social structure and local government support. The community's heterogeneity enabled collaboration around the CLT concept. The significant share of woman-headed households (>40%) also increased the model's attractiveness—the communal ownership structure increased women's access to land and capital. Local government support was also essential, alongside a considerable amount of technical assistance from planners and social workers.

Following implementation, TB-CLT's results have been mixed. TB-CLT has successfully retained affordable housing and has unified the community, fostering resident collaboration (Midheme & Moulaert, 2013). The CLT's implementation has strengthened neighbourhood stability and social networks by preventing post-project displacement. It has also extended land rights and opportunities for residents, especially women (Simonneau, Bassett, & Midheme, 2020; Taylor, 2004). The CLT has facilitated residents' access to housing finance and other resources that would not have been available otherwise.

The community has also experienced empowerment, as illustrated by four resident-established cooperatives to subsidize local housing development (Midheme & Moulaert, 2013).

TB-CLT has also faced difficulties and, arguably, failures over time—particularly in the areas of implementation and maintenance (Simonneau, Bassett, & Midheme, 2020). Administrative difficulties have been persistent, leading some to question the CLT's sustained potential (Bassett, 2005). A CLT depends on community participation, with residents contributing to the organization's management; TB-CLT has struggled to sustain its organizational structure and mandates. Central concerns include residents' unfamiliarity with the CLT model and internal leadership conflicts. Bassett (2005) reported that members of the Managing Committee were long overdue for re-election—a regular process mandated by the bylaws. However, the Managing Committee was fearful of CLT critics being elected and dissolving the original arrangement.

TB-CLT's constitutional rules have also not been enforced, including the elimination of absentee ownership (Bassett, 2005). The Managing Committee admitted they lacked the proper mechanisms to enforce absentee rules, including a contractual lease with owners that clearly stipulates TB-CLT residency (Bassett, 2005). The Managing Committee has faced a similar challenge with land sales: when a resident wishes to sell their property, the Managing Committee is limited to an advisory role and lacks appropriate oversight mechanisms. While these enforcement challenges could be addressed through strengthened land leases and property stipulations, ongoing non-compliance challenges have nurtured scepticism among local officials, weakening political support from the town and district (Bassett, 2005; Midheme & Moulaert, 2013).

3.1.2. The Caño Martín Peña CLT: San Juan, Puerto Rico

Puerto Rico's Caño Martín Peña CLT (CMP-CLT) offers a recent Global South example of the CLT model. The project grants nearly 2,000 low-income families collective ownership of 78 hectares of land (Algoed & Hernández Torrales, 2019). The CLT was established along San Juan's Martín Peña channel banks, where eight informal communities—home to 15,000-18,000 residents—were extremely vulnerable to floods (World Habitat, n.d.; Letts, 2010). In 2010, 52.5% of the total population fell below the US poverty line, with a 21.7% unemployment rate (Sheffield et al., 2014). Many houses still lack proper sanitation and water drainage (Algoed & Hernández Torrales, 2019). As part of an environmental remediation project in the late 1990s, the Puerto Rico Highway and Transportation Authority (PRHTA) broadened the effort to incorporate a comprehensive development plan (Hernández Torrales, 2007). The CLT was spawned from this process, with Martín Peña's informal communities establishing CMP-CLT as a practical response to "a strong sense of attachment to the land, persistent deprivation and fear of displacement" (Algoed & Hernández Torrales, 2019, p.32).

CMP-CLT uses a community-controlled, tripartite board of directors with eleven trustees: four residents of the Caño CLT, two residents of the Martín Peña communities, two non-residents selected based on knowledge and skills, and three representatives of governmental entities (Algoed, Hernández-Torrales, & Rodríguez Del Valle, 2018). Law-makers formalized the CLT in 2004 with Law 489, which consolidated land from several public agencies and transferred ownership to CMP-CLT in 2009 (Hernández Torrales, 2007). Shortly thereafter, CMP-CLT suffered serious setbacks: newly elected officials repealed the CLT's communal ownership, returning land to the public domain for con-ventional freehold titles (Nagy, 2017; Burkett, Verchick, & Flores, 2017). CMP-CLT's efforts to legally challenge the law were unsuccessful; however, the community's politi-cal advocacy was ultimately successful. As Nagy writes, "by the 2012 election, the Caño Martín Peña community succeeded in convincing every single mayoral and gubernatorial candidate to sign…a pledge that they would restore the land back to the trust" (2017); CMP-CLT regained land ownership in 2013.

Several factors have contributed to CMP-CLT's success, including its ability to endure serious political challenges. CMP-CLT invested heavily in public engagement and partnerships. This included a three-year community planning effort, including 700+ meetings, workshops, and public events, that sought involvement from all of CMP's res-idents (Nagy, 2017). Residents used grassroots organizing and encouraged others to think critically about their priorities, enabling community agency over their CLT (Al-goed & Hernández Torrales, 2019). Later, community empowerment was essential for confronting and, eventually, overcoming legal challenges.

CMP-CLT is an example of how to "regularize land tenure and mitigate the his-torical causes of poverty" (Algoed & Hernández Torrales, 2019, p.34); it also illustrates political and market challenges to CLTs. CMP-CLT's efforts are notable, receiving the 2015 World Habitat award for its practical and creative response to a complex housing issue (World Habitat Awards, n.d.; Williamson, 2018, 2019). The organization represents a proof-of-concept for the potential of CLTs within informal settlements in the Global South (Hernández-Torrales, Rodríguez Del Valle, Algoed, & Torres Sueiro, 2020).

4. CLTS IN INFORMAL SETTLEMENTS?

CLTs offer the potential for change in informal settlements, but how do they compare to existing policy approaches? We compare CLT attributes against existing informality policies in Table 1, demonstrating their potential to respond to a wider array of policy concerns in a more consistent manner. Unlike existing policies, the CLT offers both immediate and long-term affordability and security. Its emphasis on community control and engagement enables the CLT to retain important social networks, alongside physical improvements at the individual or community scale. However, the CLT does face legal and funding challenges. We explore this comparison in greater detail at right.

Fig. 1.1. Comparison of Informality Policies and the Community Land Trust Model

Potential Areas of Impact	Policy Models			
	Mass Social Housing	**Upgrading**	**Land Titling**	**Community Land Trust**
Immediate affordability	○ *Limited affordability to lower income populations*	● *Preservation of immediate affordability*	● *Preservation of immediate affordability*	● *Preservation of affordable housing subsidies at a unit-level through limits on resale equity and community-led ownership*
Long-term affordability and security	○ *Limited long-term affordability due to additional economic burdens such as housing maintenance, incidental expenses, taxes*	▼ *May lead to limited long-term affordability due to gentrification processes*	▼ *May lead to limited long-term affordability due to gentrification processes in cases of location advantages*	● *Guaranteed long-term affordability and security due to the removal of market speculative forces*
Infrastructure improvement	▼ *Access to better infrastructure but may lack building quality*	● *Guaranteed infrastructure improvements*	▼ *Does not necessarily include any infrastructure improvement*	▼ *Dependent on available funds*
Maintenance of existing physical and social structures	○ *Due to the relocation of residents, existing physical and social structures are not maintained*	▼ *The majority of the existing physical and social structures are maintained*	● *All physical and social structures are maintained*	● *All physical and social structures are maintained*
Potential for wealth building and reduction of poverty levels	▼ *Increased social status*	▼ *Improved living standards*	○ *It does not significantly reduce poverty levels*	● *Possibility of wealth building through low purchase costs and access to affordable loans*
Quality of life improvement	● *Positive impact on quality of life*	● *Positive impacts on living standards and quality of life*	○ *Limited quality of life improvements*	● *Potential to contribute to feelings of security, stability, and improved quality of life*
Community control	○ *No community control*	▼ *Possibility of participation but with limited community control*	▼ *Individual resident control once titles are distributed*	● *Stewarding organization and representative board ensure community control*

○, no potential for improvement or change

▼, limited potential for improvement or change

●, substantial potential improvement or change

4.1. Potential for CLTs in the Global South

In formalization projects, residents often prioritize remaining in their homes and communities (Algoed & Hernández Torrales, 2019; Williamson, 2018, 2019). Yet, a consistent challenge for existing policies is the lack of long-term affordability, security, and stability (Bredenoord & van Lindert, 2010; Comelli, Anguelovski, & Chu, 2018; Varley, 2017; Verma, 2000). The CLT's emphasis on permanent affordability and homeownership responds more directly to resident priorities, as demonstrated by CMP-CLT (Algoed & Hernández Torrales, 2019). Further, its ability to mitigate gentrification, achieved via community ownership of the land and a non-profit steward enforcing resale controls on the homes, also provides long-term security (Choi, Van Zandt, & Matarrita-Cascante, 2018; Ribeiro, 2020).

The CLT's reliance on community control, with local residents guiding and governing the non-profit owner of the underlying land, supports existing resident networks. Informal communities frequently self-organize, advocating for quality of life improvements and against eviction threats (e.g., Bremer & Bhuiyan, 2014; De Sampaio, 1994; Gay, 2010; Hardoy, Hardoy & Schusterman, 1991; Skuse & Cousins, 2007). As both cases demonstrate, CLTs offer the opportunity to leverage existing networks, providing a model that privileges community empowerment and engagement.

A central element of transformation in informal settlements is improvements to the built environment. These sites are often plagued by poor infrastructure and building conditions; they offer opportunities to adopt new building technologies, enhancing their sustainability and cost-efficiency (Wekesa, Steyn, & Otieno, 2010). CLTs provide a socio-economic framework that can adapt to a multitude of building technologies. Wekesa et. al. (2010) advocate for technologies that support in-situ upgrading without demolishing existing structures, emphasizing durability, energy consumption, and employment generation. For instance, the Affordable and Adaptable Building System and the Decentralized Processing Unit gradually improve existing environments with modular building systems that are adaptable and energy efficient (Follini et al., 2017; Hu et al., 2017; Hu et al., 2018). The CLT model enables a non-profit to educate and offer technological resources, while enabling residents to deploy sustainable building technologies that can mitigate existing conditions in a cost-effective way.

Last, CLTs explicitly support affordable ownership through a reliance on permanent subsidies, as well as a non-profit organization that facilitates access to stable loan products and homeownership education and resources (Davis, 2017). These wealth-building opportunities are particularly relevant for informal households in the Global South, as they support poverty reduction and quality of life improvements. The CLT's wealth-building structure directly refutes criticisms against existing policies, including the aestheticization of poverty (Roy, 2004) or the imposition of increased financial burdens for residents (Gilbert, 2014; Ward, 1989).

4.2. Impediments to CLTs in the Global South

CLTs face a number of obstacles that may constraint or prevent their application in informal settlements. Externally, the public sector is a central stakeholder for Global South CLTs, as highlighted in both cases. Informal settlements may occupy private or public lands, making local government support essential to securing land title. Its absence (or later revocation) can create barriers for CLTs—as CMP-CLT experienced. In the Global South, governments may resist CLTs due to common practices of clientalism—a practice where elected officials promise to provide basic needs to informal settlements in exchange for votes (Davis & White, 2012). A CLT conversion eradicates clientalist practices, formalizing ownership and eliminating dependence. Governments may also reject the possibility of CLT implementation due a refusal to give up land designated as public or government land; the assumption that only individual or corporate landholdings can generate capital surplus can also prevent governments from supporting CLTs (Alden Wily, 2020). Market pressures can also weaken political support for CLTs, especially when development is a major source of economic growth. Lack of political support can inhibit CLT land acquisition (Davis & White, 2012).

The non-uniform and unregulated nature of Global South land markets can also hinder CLT formation. Davis and White found CLTs faced the greatest resistance in informal property settings relative to formalized markets (2012). Global South cities have long histories of exploitation, inequality, and dispossession. Their contemporary political, economic, and social contexts reflect these legacies, complicating the acceptance of a process that redistributes land rights via collective ownership. Yet, these cities may also have the greatest need for land redistribution.

Internally, many CLT challenges stem from community organizing difficulties. The non-profit serves as the CLT's foundation, navigating land acquisition and homeowner sales and establishing the CLT's community-empowered mission. Establising and maintaining this community infrastructure can be difficult. CMP-CLT illustrates the importance of community ownership; its absence represents an impediment to CLTs in the Global South.

Similarly, a lack of resident consensus can inihibit the CLT's creation, as demonstrated by the Kw-amaji Urban Development Project (KUDP) in Nairobi, Kenya (Rigon, 2016). The Kwa-maji informal settlement included "high levels of tenancy, the presence of structure-owners who do not formally own land, and an informal market for structures built on public land" (Rigon, 2016, p. 2773). KUDP sought to use a CLT to gain tenure security, effectively redistributing ownership from the minority (structure-owners) to the tenant-majority (Rigon, 2016). However, the elite minority (structure-holders) opposed KUDP's reliance on collective ownership, favouring individual titles. Its failed CLT attempt shows the importance of early, sustained consensus, as well as the significance of existing power structures within informal settlements.

5. A FRAMEWORK FOR CLTS IN INFORMAL SETTLEMENTS

Based on our policy assessment, we propose a conceptual CLT framework for Global South informal settlements. A conceptual framework can offer communities, governments, practitioners, and researchers guidance on potential opportunities and challenges associated with the CLT model. The framework identifies five necessary conditions for successful CLT implementation and long-term viability (Fig. 1.2). The omission of one or more of these conditions could weaken—or even preclude—a CLT's adoption, expansion, and sustainability.

Fig. 1.2. Conceptual Framework for CLTs in Informal Settlements

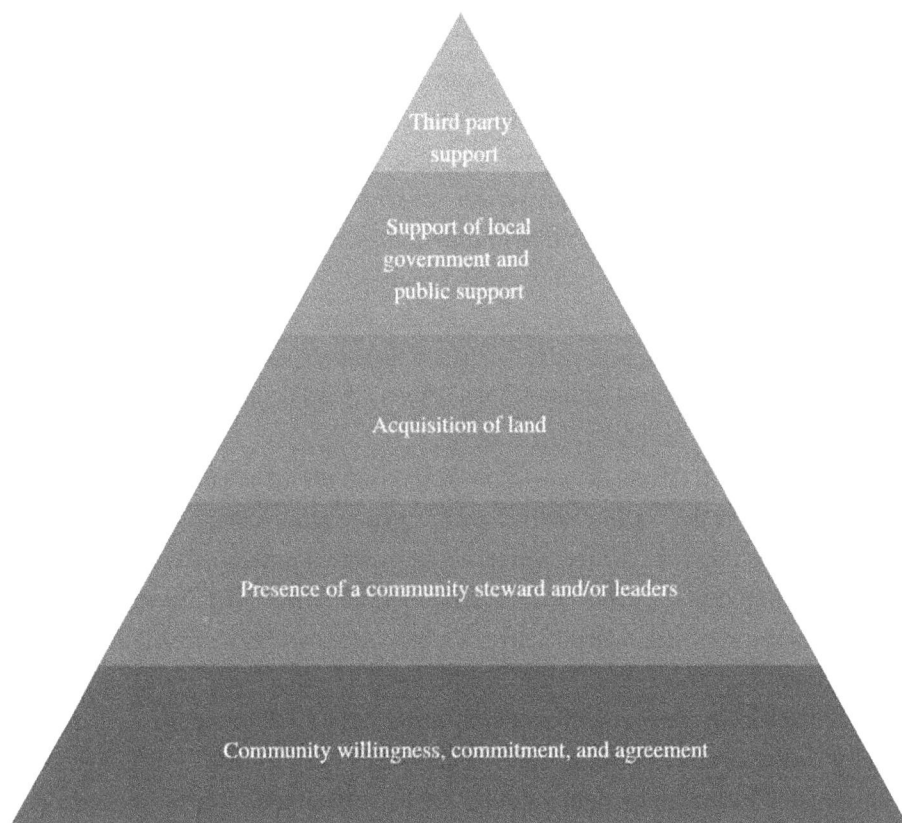

Third party
support

Support of local
government and
public support

Acquisition of land

Presence of a community steward and/or leaders

Community willingness, commitment, and agreement

Community willingness, commitment, and agreement is the first condition. This embodies a community commitment to collective ownership of land, as well as ongoing stewardship from a CLT non-profit. Given the CLT model's relative unfamiliarity, this element requires resident education and a community-led participatory process to ensure consensus. A lack of resident willingness or shared commitment to the CLT model would preclude successful CLT implementation.

The presence of a community steward and/or leaders is the second condition. CLTs require community leaders—either formal, from existing community organizations, or informal, from long-time, well-respected residents—willing to lead the process of establishing and implementing the CLT from the beginning. At the outset, community leaders or advocates would initiate the process, including CLT education, partnerships with local government and/or supporting organizations, and community advocacy. An essential goal of this process is to build sufficient community capacity and the organizational structure required to manage and maintain a community-controlled non-profit, which will serve as a long-term steward for land and housing on behalf of its residents. Following the CLT's creation, community leaders must continue to support the CLT's board and ensure broad community participation. Based on prior CLT experiences, the dearth of groups willing or able to lead—and sustain—community-led processes is a deterrent to the CLT's successful implementation.

Land acquisition is imperative to the creation of a CLT in any context; this process is distinctly different for informal settlements. There must be a real opportunity for the community to acquire the land it already occupies for the CLT to function. If political, legal, or policy circumstances prevent community acquisition, the CLT model will not work. Further, the ideal scenario allows for the CLT to acquire land without incurring substantial debt. TB-CLT and CMP-CLT both occupied acquired land from public entities; acquisition of privately-owned lands would likely require complex negotiations and financial resources. Local governments can also provide substantial financial support, leveraging existing public housing funds, grants, donations, or loans. The CLT's flexible structure enables multiple funding streams to support its work; further, individual mortgages can be supported by existing state-subsidized financing options. Over time, Global South CLTs could become self-funded, utilizing income generated by ground lease fees, house resale fees, and rental income (if the CLT develops rental housing as well as owner-occupied housing).

Public sector support represents the fourth condition, including: new legislation or amendments to existing laws (if needed), ordinances, and/or policies; the negotiation, transfer, or purchase of lands to the CLT; and/or ongoing political and financial support for the CLT model in response to resistance from the general public or special interest groups. Depending on the context, the absence of local government support may not deter a CLT project, but it does represent a significant obstacle.

Third party support is the final condition for CLT implementation. Partnerships with allied institutions, organizations, and/or technical professionals can provide critical resources that strengthen the CLT. The creation of a CLT in an informal settlement includes: (a) the establishment of a non-profit organization; (b) the adoption of CLT by-laws and mission; (c) the negotiation of land rights from public or private entities; (d) the formulation of a plan for using and developing the CLT's land, and improving infrastructure and housing; and (e) development of policies, procedures, and staff capacity within the CLT to carry out the duties of stewardship. This process can be complex, requiring technical skills related to legal processes, urban planning, and fundraising. While the absence of partnerships is not a strict impediment, it does represent a significant support, as illustrated by a number of examples.

As the non-profit is being established, third party support can aid in the development of the CLT's bylaws, operating rules, and contractual leases. The TB-CLT experience illustrates the importance of strong, enforceable lease agreements between the CLT and its homeowners; without legal protections, the CLT may struggle to protect its affordable housing clauses. Third party organizations and/or technical partners can assist the CLT in establishing legal enforcement processes and mechanisms. TB-CLT also struggled with internal conflicts over leadership that threatened the long-term viability and management of the CLT. Third party partners can represent a useful management strategy for the CLT as minority delegates on the board of directors, providing technical expertise and safeguarding CLT bylaws and democratic processes.

Third party support is also significant to the process of securing funds for the initial development, maintenance, and growth of CLTs in the Global South. Funding opportunities often include non-profits and international development organizations with directives supporting community-focused housing, as well as initiatives that support community empowerment and control. These resources are ideal targets for CLT creation and expansion in the Global South (Arrossi et al., 2013; Mitlin & Satterthwaite, 2007; Satterthwaite, 2001). For instance, a German international development organization provided funding and technical assistance for TB-CLT; CMP-CLT has received funding from a number of public and private organizations, including the Rockefeller Foundation, the Ford Foundation, and Chan Zuckerberg Initiative.

Third party actors can also provide technical and financial support to CLT homeowners, particularly through incremental infrastructure partnerships and housing microfinance programs (Ferguson & Smets, 2010). Given the predominance of incremental housing practices in informal settlements, small-scale funding pools can represent a meaningful resource to households. Financial partnerships can help the CLT establish affordable financing options, including no-interest or low-interest loans through a revolving loan fund or a community-based housing loan fund. In addition, partnerships can support the CLT's efforts to provide financial counseling and entrepreneurship support in service of existing infrastructure improvement, home maintenance, and wealth-building.

6. CONCLUSIONS

There is no "one-size-fits all" policy model to address urban informality in the Global South. Informal settlements are heterogeneous and exist in diverse contexts. Accordingly, policy responses need to be varied to respond to the complexity of informal settlements (Walker, 2016). Legacies of power imabalances and dispossesion have long dictated property rights in the Global South. The CLT model offers one response to diminish the long-lasting consequences of such processes.

We have examined the potential of and impediments to the CLT model in the Global South, assessing it against three existing policy responses to informal settlements—mass social housing, upgrading, and individual land titling. Subsequently, we proposed a conceptual framework that outlines the necessary conditions for a CLT within the Global South. This framework is relevant for stakeholders interested in alternate responses to informality, in addition to expanding the conversation about CLT replicability within the Global South.

As a bottom-up model, the CLT does not represent a standard approach to housing and community development. By nature, it relies on a highly collaborative process that limits the decision-making role(s) for government and traditional power structures. Accordingly, the decision to pursue a CLT rests with the community itself. While governments can provide the legal infrastructure, educational resources, and, potentially, seed funding to enable communities to take ownership of their land, they cannot force a CLT process. Communities must retain agency over the CLT, thereby limiting the role of government in its development.

Although TB-CLT and CMP-CLT offer valuable insights, CLTs have heretofore been absent from most of the policy discourse surrounding informal settlements. There is a need for increased CLT research within the Global South, examining in particular the long-term benefits or drawbacks of the model for residents and the surrounding communities. Every policy model has its own advantages and disadvantages. Context matters. CLTs are not the ultimate response to informality, but another tool in the toolbox for informal settlements—one with the ability to offer permanently affordable housing, wealth building opportunities, quality of life improvements, and community control over the use and development of land. It is a tool for ensuring the improvement of informal settlements without the displacement of its most vulnerable residents.

Notes

1. This essay originally appeared in Habitat International, Vol 96/102108, Patricia Basile and Meagan M. Ehlenz, "Examining Responses to Informality in the Global South: A Framework for Community Land Trusts and Informal Settlements," copyright 2020. It is reprinted here with the permission of Elsevier.

2. Regularization policies focus primarily on formalizing the rights to use and own the land occupied by informal settlements' residents. Approaches to land regularization have varied in different countries and contexts. See Fernandes (2011) for a review of the two primary paradigms for regularization programs.

3. Mass social housing in the Global South is a strategy focused on promoting individual homeownership to low-income families. The approach includes the construction of mass-produced housing complexes, alongside financial subsidies to enable qualified

households to purchase a dwelling unit. Whereas mass social housing (i.e., public housing) in the Global North predominately emphasizes subsidized rental assistance for low-income households, many countries in Africa and Latin America have promoted homeownership through finance-driven social housing programs.

References

Abrams, C. (1966). *Squatter settlements: the problem and the opportunity* (No. 63). Office of International Affairs, Dept. of Housing and Urban Development.

Acolin, A., & Green, R. K. (2017). Measuring housing affordability in São Paulo metropolitan region: Incorporating location. *Cities, 62*, 41–49. *https://doi.org/10.1016/j .cities.2016.12.003.*

Aernouts & Ryckewaert. (2018). Beyond Housing: On the Role of Commoning in the Establishment of a Community Land Trust Project. *International Journal of Housing Policy, 18* (4), 503–21. *https://doi.org/10.1080/19491247.2017.1331592.*

Agamben, G. (1998). *Homo sacer: Sovereign power and bare life.* Stanford University Press.

Alden Wily, L. (2020). Challenges for the New Kid on the Block—Collective Property. In J.E. Davis, L. Algoed, & M.E. Hernández-Torrales (Eds.), *On Common Ground: International Perspectives on the Community Land Trust* (pp. 63–71). Madison: Terra Nostra Press.

Algoed, L., Hernández Torrales, M.E., & Rodríguez Del Valle, L.N. (2018). *El Fideicomiso de la Tierra del Caño Martín Peña: Instrumento Notable de Regularización de Suelo en Asentamientos Informales.* Lincoln Institute of Land Policy. Retrieved from *https:// www.lincolninst.edu.publications/working-papers/el-fideicomiso-la-tierra-del-cano- martin-pena.*

Algoed, L., & Hernández Torrales, M. E. (2019). The land is ours. Vulnerabilization and resistance in informal settlements in Puerto Rico: Lessons from the Caño Martín Peña Community Land Trust. *Radical Housing Journal, 1*(1), 29–47.

AlSayyad, N. (2004). Urban informality as a 'new'way of life. In A. Roy, & N. AlSayyad (Eds.), *Urban Informality: Transnational Perspectives from the Middle East, Latin America, and South Asia* (pp. 7–30). New York: Lexington Books.

Aristizabal, N., & Gomez, A. O. (2002). Are services more important than titles in Bogotá? In G.K. Payne (Ed.), *Land, Rights and Innovation: Improving Tenure Security for the Urban Poor* (pp. 100–113). Practical Action Publishing.

Arrossi, S., Bombarolo, F., Hardoy, J. E., Mitlin, D., Coscio, L. P., & Satterthwaite, D. (2013). *Funding Community Initiatives.* New York: Earthscan.

Atuesta, L. H., & Soares, Y. (2018). Urban upgrading in Rio de Janeiro: Evidence from the Favela-Bairro programme. *Urban Studies, 55*(1), 53–70. *https://doi.org/10.1177 /0042098016669290.*

Balchin, P. (Ed.). (2013). *Housing Policy in Europe*. London: Routledge.

Bassett, E. M., & Jacobs, H. M. (1997). Community-based tenure reform in urban Africa: the community land trust experiment in Voi, Kenya. *Land Use Policy, 14*(3), 215-229. *https://doi.org/10.1016/S0264-8377(97)00003-3.*

Bassett, E. M. (2005). Tinkering with tenure: the community land trust experiment in Voi, Kenya. *Habitat International, 29*(3), 375–398. *https://doi.org/10.1016/j.habitatint. 2003.12.001.*

Bassett, E. M. (2007). The persistence of the commons: Economic theory and community decision-making on land tenure in Voi, Kenya. *African Studies Quarterly, 9*(3), 1–29.

Berriane, Y. (2010). The complexities of inclusive participatory governance: The case of Moroccan: Associational life in the context of the INDH. *Journal of Economic and Social Research, 12*(1), 89-111.

Bredenoord, J., & van Lindert, P. (2010). Pro-poor housing policies: Rethinking the potential of assisted self-help housing. *Habitat International, 34*(3), 278-287. *https://doi. org/10.1016/j.habitatint.2009.12.001.*

Bremer, J., & Bhuiyan, S. H. (2014). Community-led infrastructure development in informal areas in urban Egypt: A case study. *Habitat International, 44*, 258–267. *https://doi. org/10.1016/j.habitatint.2014.07.004.*

Briggs, J. (2011). The land formalisation process and the peri-urban zone of Dar es Salaam, Tanzania. *Planning Theory and Practice, 12*(1), 115-153. *https://doi.org/10.1080/ 14649357.2011.545626.*

Buckley, R.M., Kallergis, A. & Wainer, L. (2016). The emergence of large-scale housing programs: Beyond a public finance perspective. *Habitat International, 54*(3), 199–209. *https://doi.org/10.1016/j.habitatint.2015.11.022.*

Bunce, S. 2016. "Pursuing Urban Commons: Politics and Alliances in Community Land Trust Activism in East London." *Antipode, 48*(1), 134–50. *https://doi.org/10.1111/ anti.12168.*

Burgess, R. (1978). Petty commodity housing or dweller control? A critique of John Turner's views on housing policy. *World Development, 6*(9-10), 1105–1133. *https://doi.org/ 10.1016/0305-750X(78)90067-0.*

Burkett, M., Verchick, R. R. M., & Flores, D. (2017). *Reaching higher ground avenues to secure and manage new land for communities displaced by climate change.* Center for Progressive Reform. Retrieved from: *http://progressivereform.org/articles/ReachingHigher-Ground_1703.pdf.* Accessed 8 August 2019.

Butala, N. M., VanRooyen, M. J., & Patel, R. B. (2010). Improved health outcomes in urban slums through infrastructure upgrading. *Social Science & Medicine, 71*(5), 935–940. *https://doi.org/10.1016/j.socscimed.2010.05.037.*

Cabré, E., & Andrés, A. (2018). La Borda: A case study on the implementation of cooperative housing in Catalonia. *International Journal of Housing Policy, 18*(3), 412–32. h*ttps://doi. org/10.1080/19491247.2017.1331591*.

Choi, M., Van Zandt, S., & Matarrita-Cascante, D. (2018). Can community land trusts slow gentrification? *Journal of Urban Affairs, 40*(3), 394–411. *https://doi.org/10.1080/0735 2166.2017.1362318*.

Cohen, M. (2001). Urban assistance and the material world: learning by doing at the World Bank. *Environment and Urbanization, 13*(1), 37-60. *https://doi.org/10.1177/09562 4780101300104*.

Comelli, T., Anguelovski, I., & Chu, E. (2018). Socio-spatial legibility, discipline, and gentri-fication through favela upgrading in Rio de Janeiro. *City, 22*(5-6), 633–656. *https://doi. org/10.1080/13604813.2018.1549205*.

Crabtree, L. (2006). Sustainability begins at home? An ecological exploration of sub/urban Australian community-focused housing initiatives. *Geoforum, 37*(4): 519–535. *https:// doi.org/10.1016/j.geoforum.2005.04.002*.

da Costa, A. A., & do Nascimento, E. A. (2016). A produção de espaço urbano e os fatores do processo de expansão do mercado imobiliário em Mossoró-RN [The production of urban space and the factors of the process of expansion of the real estate market in Mos-soró-RN]. *Ateliê Geográfico, 10*(2), 21-41. *https://doi.org/10.5216/ag.v10i2.33631*.

da Silva Telles, V. (2010). Nas dobras do legal e do ilegal: Ilegalismos e jogos de poder nas tramas da cidade [In the folds of the legal and the illegal: Illegalisms and power games in the webs of the city]. *Dilemas: Revista de Estudos de Conflito e Controle, 2*(5/6), 97–126.

Davis, D. E. &White, M. (2012). El fideicomiso de propiedad comunitaria como recurso para reducir la pobreza urbana: ¿Pueden los derechos a la propiedad colectiva ser la clave para alcanzar un future incluyente y socialmente sustentable en la ciudad?. In Ziccardi. A. (Ed.), Ciudades del 2010: Entre la Sociedad del Conocimiento y la Desigualdad Social. Vol. 1. (pp. 403–457). Mexico: National Autonomous University of Mexico/PUEC.

Davis, J. E. (2010a). More than money: What is shared in shared equity homeownership? *Journal of Affordable Housing and Community Development Law, 19* (3 & 4), 259–77.

Davis, J. E. (2010b). *The Community Land Trust Reader*. Cambridge, MA: Lincoln Institute of Land Policy.

Davis, J. E. (2017). *Affordable For Good: Building Inclusive Communities Through Homes That Last. Shelter Report.* Washington, D.C.: Habitat for Humanity.

Davis, M. (2006). Planet of slums. *New Perspectives Quarterly, 23*(2), 6-11. *https://doi.org/ 10.1111/j.1540-5842.2006.00797.x*.

de Duren, N. R. L. (2018a). Why there? Developers' rationale for building social housing in the urban periphery in Latin America. *Cities, 72,* 411–420. *https://doi.org/10.1016/j.cities.2017.10.006.*

de Duren, N. R. (2018b). The social housing burden: comparing households at the periphery and the centre of cities in Brazil, Colombia, and Mexico. *International Journal of Housing Policy, 18*(2), 177–203. *https://doi.org/10.1080/19491247.2017.1298366.*

De Geest, F., & De Nys-Ketels, S. (2019). Everyday resistance: Exposing the complexities of participatory slum-upgrading projects in Nagpur. *Housing Studies, 34*(10), 1673–1689. *https://doi.org/10.1080/02673037.2018.1562056.*

De Sampaio, M. R. A. (1994). Community organization, housing improvements and income generation: A case study of 'Favelas' in São Paulo, Brazil. *Habitat International, 18*(4), 81–97. *https://doi.org/10.1016/0197-3975(94)90019-1.*

De Soto, H. (2000). *The Mystery Of Capital: Why Capitalism Triumphs In The West And Fails Everywhere Else.* London: Bantam Press.

De Souza, F. A. (2001). The future of informal settlements: Lessons in the legalization of disputed urban land in Recife, Brazil. *Geoforum, 32*(4), 483–492. *https://doi.org/10.1016/S0016-7185(01)00014-8.*

DeFilippis, J., Stromberg, B., & Williams, O. R. (2018). W(h)ither the community in community land trusts?" *Journal of Urban Affairs 40*(6): 755–69. *https://doi.org/10.1080/07352166.2017.1361302.*

Deinlnger, K., & Binswanger, H. (1999). The evolution of the World Bank's land policy: principles, experience, and future challenges. *The World Bank Research Observer, 14*(2), 247–276. *https://doi.org/10.1093/wbro/14.2.247.*

Durand-Lasserve, A. (2006). Informal settlements and the millennium development goals: Global policy debates on property ownership and security of tenure. *Global Urban Development, 2*(1), 1–15.

Ehlenz, M. M. (2014). Managing the land access paradox in the urbanising world. *Critical Housing Analysis 1*(1), 17–25. Retrieved from *http://www.housing-critical.com/home-page-1/managing-the-land-access-paradox-in-the-urbaniz.*

Ehlenz, M. M. (2018). Making home more affordable: Community land trusts adopting cooperative ownership models to expand affordable housing. *Journal of Community Practice, 26*(3): 283–307. *https://doi.org/10.1080/10705422.2018.1477082.*

Ehlenz, M. M., & Taylor, C. (2019). Shared equity homeownership in the United States: A literature review. *Journal of Planning Literature, 34*(1), 3–18. *https://doi.org/10.1177/0885412218795142.*

Ferguson, B., & Smets, P. (2010). Finance for incremental housing; current status and prospects for expansion. *Habitat International, 34*(3), 288–298. *https://doi.org/10.1016/j.habitatint.2009.11.008.*

Fernandes, E., & Varley, A.(1998). *Illegal Cities: Law and Urban Change in Developing Countries.* London: Zed Books.

Fernandes, E. (2011). *Regularization of Informal Settlements in Latin America.* Cambridge, MA: Lincoln Institute of Land Policy.

Follini, C., Hu, R., Pan, W., Linner, T., & Bock, T. (2017). Collaborative Advanced Building Methodology toward Industrialization of Informal Settlements in Cairo. In *Proceedings of the 34th International Symposium on Automation and Robotics in Construction (ISARC).*

Galiani, S., & Schargrodsky, E. (2010). Property rights for the poor: Effects of land titling. *Journal of Public Economics, 94*(9–10), 700-729. *https://doi.org/10.1016/j.jpubeco.2010.06.002.*

Gay, R. (2010). *Popular Organization and Democracy on Rio De Janeiro: A Tale of Two Favelas.* Philadelphia, PA: Temple University Press.

Gilbert, A. (1990). The costs and benefits of illegality and irregularity in the supply of land. In J.J. van der Linden & P. Baross (Eds.). *The Transformation of Land Supply Systems in Third World Cities* (pp. 17–36). Aldershot, UK: Avebury.

Gilbert, A. (2001). *Housing in Latin America.* Inter-American Development Bank.

Gilbert, A. (2002). On the mystery of capital and the myths of Hernando de Soto: What difference does legal title make? *International Development Planning Review, 24*(1), 1–19. *https://doi.org/10.3828/idpr.24.1.1.*

Gilbert, R. (2003). *Improving the Lives of the Poor Through Investment in Cities: An Update on the Performance of the World Bank's Urban Portfolio.* Washington, D.C.: The World Bank. Retrieved from *http://documents.worldbank.org/curated/en/665271468781814799/pdf/289840PAPER0Im1ves01see0also0258991.pdf.* Accessed 5 August 2019.

Gilbert, A. (2012). de Soto's the Mystery of Capital: Reflections on the book's public impact. *International Development Planning Review, 34*(3), pp.v–xviii. *https://doi.org/10.3828/idpr.2012.15.*

Gilbert, A. G. (2014). Free housing for the poor: An effective way to address poverty? *Habitat International, 41,* 253–261. *https://doi.org/10.1016/j.habitatint.2013.08.009.*

Gulyani, S., & Bassett, E. M. (2007). Retrieving the baby from the bathwater: Slum upgrading in Sub-Saharan Africa. *Environment and Planning C: Government and Policy, 25*(4), 486–515. *https://doi.org/10.1068/c4p.*

Hardoy, A., Hardoy, J. E., & Schusterman, R. (1991). Building community organization: the history of a squatter settlement and its own organizations in Buenos Aires. *Environment and Urbanization, 3*(2), 104–120. *https://doi.org/10.1177/095624789100300215.*

Handzic, K. (2010). Is legalized land tenure necessary in slum upgrading? Learning from Rio's land tenure policies in the Favela Bairro Program. *Habitat International, 34*(1), 11–17. *https://doi.org/10.1016/j.habitatint.2009.04.001.*

Hernández-Torrales, M.E. (2007). The Caño Martín Peña Community Land Trust: Corollary of a model of community involvement. *Progress, Revista del Colegio de Abogados de Puerto Rico, 68*(4), 794–817.

Hernández-Torrales, M.E., Rodríguez Del Valle, L., Algoed, L., & Torres Sueiro, K. (2020). Seeding the CLT in Latin America and the Caribbean: Origins, Achievements, and the Proof-of-Concept Example of the Caño Martín Peña Community Land Trust. In J.E. Davis, L. Algoed, & M.E. Hernández-Torrales (Eds.), *On Common Ground: International Perspectives on the Community Land Trust* (pp.189–210). Madison: Terra Nostra Press.

Hu, R., Follini, C., Pan, W., Linner, T., & Bock, T. (2017). A case study on regenerating informal settlements in Cairo using Affordable and Adaptable Building System. Procedia engineering, 196, 113–120. *https://doi.org/10.1016/j.proeng.2017.07.180.*

Hu, R., Linner, T., Follini, C., Pan, W., & Bock, T. (2018). An Affordable and Adaptable Building System to Transform Informal Settlements in Cairo. In *Proceedings of S. ARCH International Architecture Conference.*

Hylton, E., & Charles, K. J. (2018). Informal mechanisms to regularize informal settlements: Water services in São Paulo's favelas. *Habitat International, 80,* 41–48. *https://doi.org/10.1016/j.habitatint.2018.07.010.*

Imparato, I., & Ruster, J. (2003). *Slum Upgrading and Participation: Lessons from Latin America.* The World Bank.

Institute for Community Economics. 1982. *The Community Land Trust Handbook.* Emmaus, PA: Rodale Press.

Jacobus, R., & Davis, J. E. (2010). *The Asset Building Potential of Shared Equity Home Ownership.* New America Foundation. Retrieved from *https://community-wealth.org/content/asset-building-potential-shared-equity-home-ownership-0.* Accessed 13 August 2019.

Johnson, Jr, T. E. (1987). Upward filtering of housing stock: A study of upward filtering of housing stock as a consequence of informal settlement upgrading in developing countries. *Habitat International, 11*(1), 173–190. *https://doi.org/10.1016/0197-3975(87)90046-4.*

Kagawa, A., & Turkstra, J. (2002). The process of urban land tenure formalisation in Peru. In In G.K. Payne (Ed.), *Land, Rights and Innovation: Improving Tenure Security for the Urban Poor* (pp. 19–33). Practical Action Publishing.

Keare, D. H., & Parris, S. (1982). *Evaluation of Shelter Programs for the Urban Poor.* Washington, D.C.: World Bank.

Kiddle, G. L. (2010). Key theory and evolving debates in international housing policy: From legalisation to perceived security of tenure approaches. *Geography Compass, 4*(7), 881–892. *https://doi.org/10.1111/j.1749-8198.2010.00340.x.*

Kiefer, K., & Ranganathan, M. (2018). The politics of participation in cape Town's slum upgrading: the role of productive tension. *Journal of Planning Education and Research,* 1–15. *https://doi.org/10.1177/0739456X18761119.*

Kironde, J. L. (2006). The regulatory framework, unplanned development and urban poverty: Findings from Dar es Salaam, Tanzania. *Land Use Policy, 23*(4), 460–472. *https://doi.org/10.1016/j.landusepol.2005.07.004.*

Kowaltowski, D., Granja, A. D., Moreira, D. D. C., Pina, S. M., Oliva, C. A., & Castro, M. R. (2015). The Brazilian housing program. *Journal of the Korean Housing Association, 26*(6), 35–42. *https://doi.org/10.6107/jkha.2015.26.6.035.*

Kowaltowski, D. C., Muianga, E. A. D., Granja, A. D., Moreira, D. D. C., Bernardini, S. P., & Castro, M. R. (2019). A critical analysis of research of a mass-housing programme. *Building Research & Information, 47*(6), 716–733. *https://doi.org/10.1080/09613218.2018.1458551.*

Lang, R., & Stoeger, H. (2018). The role of the local institutional context in understanding collaborative housing models: Empirical evidence from Austria. *International Journal of Housing Policy 18*(1), 35–54. *https://doi.org/10.1080/19491247.2016.1265265.*

Lee-Smith, D., & Memon, P. A. (1988). Institution development for delivery of low-income housing: an evaluation of the Dandora Community Development Project in Nairobi. *Third World Planning Review, 10*(3), 217–238. *https://doi.org/10.3828/twpr.10.3.r28q530672721r44.*

Letts, C. (2010). Community (dis)empowerment: The Cano Martin Pena Project. *Harvard Journal of Hispanic Policy, 22,* 65–71.

Macedo, J. (2010). Methodology adaptation across levels of development: Applying a US regional housing model to Brazil. *Housing Studies, 25*(5), 607–624. *https://doi.org/10.1080/02673037.2010.483582.*

Mangin, W. (1967). Latin American squatter settlements: a problem and a solution. *Latin American Research Review, 2*(3), 65–98.

Marais, L., & Ntema, J. (2013). The upgrading of an informal settlement in South Africa: Two decades onwards. *Habitat International, 39,* 85–95. *https://doi.org/10.1016/j.habitatint.2012.11.001.*

Martin, D. G., Esfahani, A. H., Williams, O. R., Kruger, R., Pierce, J., & DeFilippis, J. (2019). Meanings of limited equity homeownership in community land trusts. *Housing Studies.* *https://doi.org/10.1080/02673037.2019.1603363.*

Mastrodi, J., & Zaccara, S. M. L. S. (2016). Sobre a promoção do direito à moradia: um estudo à luz da política urbana do município de Campinas [On the promotion of the right to housing: a study on the nature of urban policy in Campinas]. *Revista de Direito da Cidade, 8*(1), 1–28.

McAuslan, P. (1985). *Urban land and shelter for the poor.* London: Earthscan.

McBride, B., & French, M. (2011). *Affordable Land and Housing in Latin America and the Caribbean.* Nairobi: United Nations Human Settlements Program.

McFarlane, C. (2008). Sanitation in Mumbai's informal settlements: State, 'slum', and infra-structure. *Environment and Planning A, 40*(1), 88–107. *https://doi.org/10.1068/a39221.*

Mensah, C. A., Andres, L., Baidoo, P., Eshun, J. K., & Antwi, K. B. (2017). Community partic-ipation in urban planning: The case of managing green spaces in Kumasi, Ghana. *Urban Forum, 28*(2), 125–141. *https://doi.org/10.1007/s12132-016-9295-7.*

Midheme, E., & Moulaert, F. (2013). Pushing back the frontiers of property: Community land trusts and low-income housing in urban Kenya. *Land Use Policy, 35,* 73–84. *https://doi.org/10.1016/j.landusepol.2013.05.005.*

Minnery, J., Argo, T., Winarso, H., Hau, D., Veneracion, C. C., Forbes, D., & Childs, I. (2013). Slum upgrading and urban governance: Case studies in three South East Asian cities. *Habitat International, 39,* 162–169. *https://doi.org/10.1016/j.habitatint.2012.12.002.*

Mitlin, D., & Satterthwaite, D. (2007). Strategies for grassroots control of international aid. *Environment and Urbanization, 19*(2), 483–500. h*ttps://doi.org/10.1177/0956247807082831.*

Moura, J. M. D. (2014). "Minha Casa, Minha Vida" program at the Metropolitan Region of Natal: A sociospatial analysis of the impact of the segregation and deterritorialization. urbe. *Revista Brasileira de Gestão Urbana, 6*(3), 339–359. *http://dx.doi.org/10.7213/urbe.06.003.AC05.*

Mullins, D., & Moore, T. (2018). Self-organised and civil society participation in housing provision. *International Journal of Housing Policy 18*(1), 1–14. *https://doi.org/10.1080/19491247.2018.1422320.*

Nagy, C. (2017). El Caño Vive, La Lucha Sigue! Community-controlled land in Puerto Rico. *Shelterforce.* Retrieved from *https://shelterforce.org/2017/03/27/el-cano-vive-la-lucha-sigue-community-controlled-land-in-puerto-rico/.* Accessed 13 August 2019.

National Community Land Trust Network. (n.d.). Program directory. *National Community Land Trust Network. Retrieved from http://cltnetwork.org/directory/.* Accessed 15 August 2019.

Panaritis, E. (2007). *Prosperity Unbound: Building Property Markets With Trust.* Basingstoke: Palgrave Macmillan.

Payne, G., Durand-Lasserve, A., & Rakodi, C. (2009). The limits of land titling and home ownership. *Environment and Urbanization, 21*(2), 443–462. *https://doi.org/10.1177/0956247809344364.*

Payne, G. (2001). Urban land tenure policy options: Titles or rights? *Habitat International, 25*(3), 415–429. *https://doi.org/10.1016/S0197-3975(01)00014-5.*

Peattie, L. R. (1982). Some second thoughts on sites-and-services. *Habitat International, 6* (1–2), 131–139. *https://doi.org/10.1016/0197-3975(82)90054-6.*

Peek, O., Hordijk, M., & d'Auria, V. (2018). User-based design for inclusive urban transformation: Learning from 'informal' and 'formal' dwelling practices in Guayaquil, Ecuador. *International Journal of Housing Policy, 18*(2), 204–232. *https://doi.org/10.1080/19491247.2016.1265268.*

Perlman, J. (2016). The formalization of informal real estate transactions in Rio's favelas. In E.L. Birch, S. Chattaraj, & S. M. Wachter (Eds.), *Slums: How Informal Real Estate Markets Work* (pp. 58–82). Philadelphia, PA: University of Pennsylvania Press.

Rappaport, J. (2010). The effectiveness of homeownership in building household wealth. *Federal Reserve Bank of Kansas City Economic Review, 95*(4), 35–65.

Retsinas, N.P., & Belsky, E.S. (Eds.). (2004). *Low-income homeownership: Examining the unexamined goal.* Washington, DC: Brookings Institution Press.

Ribeiro, T. F. (2020). Os "Community Land Trusts": potencialidades e desafios de sua implementação nas cidades brasileiras. *Revista de Direito da Cidade, 12*(1), 609–631.

Rigon, A. (2016). Collective or individual titles? Conflict over tenure regularisation in a Kenyan informal settlement. *Urban Studies, 53*(13), 2758–2778. *https://doi.org/10.1177/0042098015602658.*

Rolnik, R. (2013a). Late neoliberalism: The financialization of homeownership and housing rights. *International Journal of Urban and Regional Research, 37*(3), 1058–1066. *https://doi.org/10.1111/1468-2427.12062.*

Rolnik, R. (2013b). Ten years of the City Statute in Brazil: From the struggle for urban reform to the World Cup cities. *International Journal of Urban Sustainable Development, 5*(1), 54–64. *https://doi.org/10.1080/19463138.2013.782706.*

Roy, A. (2003). *City requiem, Calcutta: gender and the politics of poverty.* Minneapolis, MN: U of Minnesota Press.

Roy, A. (2004). Transnational trespassings: The geopolitics of urban informality. In A. Roy, & N. AlSayyad (Eds.), *Urban Informality: Transnational Perspectives from the Middle East, Latin America, and South Asia* (pp. 289–317). New York: Lexington Books.

Roy, A. (2005). Urban informality: Toward an epistemology of planning. *Journal of the American Planning Association, 71*(2), 147–158. *https://doi.org/10.1080/01944360508976689.*

Rufino, M. B. C. (2016). Transformação da periferia e novas formas de desigualdades nas metrópoles brasileiras: Um olhar sobre as mudanças na produção habitacional [Peripheral transformation and new forms of inequality in Brazilian metropolises: A look at changes in housing production]. *Cadernos Metrópole, 18*(35), 217–236. *https://doi.org/10.1590/2236-9996.2016-3510.*

Sanyal, B. (1996). Intention and outcome: formalization and its consequences. *Regional Development Dialogue, 17,* 161–178.

Satterthwaite, D. (2001). Reducing urban poverty: constraints on the effectiveness of aid agencies and development banks and some suggestions for change. *Environment and Urbanization, 13*(1), 137–157. *https://doi.org/10.1177/095624780101300111*

Simonneau, C., Bassett, E., & Midheme, E. (2020). Seeding the CLT in Africa: Lessons from the Early Efforts to Establish Community Land Trusts in Kenya. In J.E. Davis, L. Algoed, & M.E. Hernández-Torrales (Eds.), *On Common Ground: International Perspectives on the Community Land Trust* (pp. 245–261). Madison: Terra Nostra Press.

Sheffield, P.E., Agu D.P., Rowe, M., Fischer, K., Pérez, A.E., Rodríguez, L.N., & Avilés, K.R. (2014). *Health Impact Assessment of the Proposed Environmental Restoration of Caño Martín Peña. San Juan, Puerto Rico.* Retrieved from *https://www.pewtrusts.org/-/media/assets/external-sites/health-impact-project/mssm-hia-report.pdf.* Accessed 11 November 2019.

Shirgaokar, M., & Rumbach, A. (2018). Investigating housing tenures beyond homeownership: a study of informal settlements in Kolkata, India. *Housing Studies, 33*(1), 117–139. *https://doi.org/10.1080/02673037.2017.1344955.*

Sholder, H. & Arif Hasan (2020). The Origins and Evolution of the CLT Model in South Asia. In J.E. Davis, L. Algoed, & M.E. Hernández-Torrales (Eds.), *On Common Ground: International Perspectives on the Community Land Trust* (pp.263–280). Madison: Terra Nostra Press.

Shortt, N. K., & Hammett, D. (2013). Housing and health in an informal settlement upgrade in Cape Town, South Africa. *Journal of Housing and the Built Environment, 28*(4), 615–627. *https://doi.org/10.1007/s10901-013-9347-4.*

Silva, P. C., & Mautner, Y. (2016). Tenure regularization programs in favelas in Brazil. In E.L. Birch, S. Chattaraj, & S. M. Wachter (Eds.), *Slums: How informal real estate markets work* (pp. 83–93). Philadelphia, PA: University of Pennsylvania Press.

Sims, D. (2002). What is secure tenure in urban Egypt? In G.K. Payne (Ed.), *Land, Rights and Innovation: Improving Tenure Security for the Urban Poor* (pp. 77–99). Practical Action Publishing.

Skuse, A., & Cousins, T. (2007). Spaces of resistance: Informal settlement, communication and community organisation in a Cape Town township. *Urban Studies, 44*(5–6), 979–995. *https://doi.org/10.1080/00420980701256021.*

Syagga, P. M. (2006). Land ownership and use in Kenya: policy prescriptions from an inequality perspective. *Readings on Inequality in Kenya. Sectoral Dynamics and Perspectives, Nairobi,* 289–344.

Taylor, W. E. (2004). Property rights—and responsibilities? The case of Kenya. *Habitat International, 28*(2), 275–87. *https://doi.org/10.1016/S0197-3975(03)00073-0.*

Temkin, K. M., Theodos, B., & Price, D. (2010). Balancing affordability and opportunity: An evaluation of affordable homeownership programs with long-term affordability controls. *The Urban Institute.* Retrieved from *http://www.urban.org/sites/default/files/publication/29291/412244-Balancing-Affordability-and-Opportunity-An-Evaluation-of-Affordable-Homeownership-Programs-with-Long-term-Affordability-Controls.PDF.* Accessed 5 August 2019.

Temkin, K. M., Theodos, B., & Price, D. (2013). Sharing equity with future generations: An evaluation of long-term affordable homeownership programs in the USA. *Housing Studies, 28*(4), 553–78. *https://doi.org/10.1080/02673037.2013.759541.*

Thaden, E., & Rosenberg, G. (2010). Outperforming the market: Delinquency and foreclosure rates in community land trusts. *Land Lines Magazine.* Retrieved from *https://www.lincolninst.edu/publications/articles/outperforming-market.* Accessed 20 August 2019.

Thaden, E. (2011). "Stable Home Ownership in a Turbulent Economy: Delinquencies and Foreclosure Remain Low in Community Land Trusts." *Lincoln Institute of Land Policy.* Retrieved from *http://www.lincolninst.edu/sites/default/files/pubfiles/1936_1257_thaden_final.pdf.* Accessed 20 August 2019.

Thaden, E., Greer, A., & Saegert, S. (2013). Shared equity homeownership: A welcomed tenure alternative among lower income households. *Housing Studies, 28*(8), 1175–96. *https://doi.org/10.1080/02673037.2013.818621.*

Theodos, B., Pitingolo, R., Latham, S., Stacy, C., Daniels, R., & B. Braga. (2017). Affordable Homeownership: An Evaluation of Shared Equity Programs. *Urban Institute.* Retrieved from *https://www.nationalservice.gov/sites/default/files/evidenceexchange/FR_CHIP%20Final%20Report_2017.pdf.* Accessed 20 August 2019.

Turley, R., Saith, R., Bhan, N., Rehfuess, E., & Carter, B. (2013). Slum upgrading strategies involving physical environment and infrastructure interventions and their effects on health and socio-economic outcomes. Cochrane Database of Systematic Reviews, 35(1), 171–175. *https://doi.org/10.1002/14651858.CD010067.pub2.*

Turner, J. C. (1968). Housing priorities, settlement patterns, and urban development in modernizing countries. Journal of the American Institute of Planners, 34(6), 354–363. *https://doi.org/10.1080/01944366808977562.*

Turner, J. F. (1972). Housing as a verb. In J. F. Turner & R. Fichter (Eds.), Freedom to build, (pp. 48–175). Macmillan.

Ukoje, J. E., & Kanu, K. U. (2014). Implementation and the challenges of the mass housing scheme in Abuja, Nigeria. *American International Journal of Contemporary Research*, 4(4), 209–218.

U.N. Habitat. (2016). Slum almanac 2015–2016: Tracking improvement in the lives of slum dwellers. Participatory Slum Upgrading Programme.

Van Gelder, J. L. (2010). What tenure security? The case for a tripartite view. *Land use policy*, 27(2), 449–456.

Valença, M. M., & Bonates, M. F. (2010). The trajectory of social housing policy in Brazil: From the National Housing Bank to the Ministry of the Cities. Habitat International, 34(2), 165–173. *https://doi.org/10.1016/j.habitatint.2009.08.006.*

van Lindert, P. (2016). Rethinking urban development in Latin America: A review of changing paradigms and policies. Habitat International, 54, 253–264. *https://doi.org/ 10.1016/j.habitatint.2015.11.017.*

Varley, A. (1987). The relationship between tenure legalization and housing improvements: evidence from Mexico City. Development and Change, 18, 463–481. *https://doi. org/10.1111/j.1467-7660.1987.tb00281.x.*

Varley, A., 2002. Private or public: debating the meaning of tenure legalization. International Journal of Urban and Regional Research, 26(3), 449–461. *https://doi.org/10.1111 /1468-2427.00392.*

Varley, A. (2017). Property titles and the urban poor: from informality to displacement? *Planning Theory & Practice*, 18(3), 385–404. *https://doi.org/10.1080/14649357.2016 .1235223.*

Verma, G. D. (2000). Indore's Habitat Improvement Project: success or failure? Habitat International, 24(1), 91–117. *https://doi.org/10.1016/S0197-3975(99)00031-4.*

Vuong, T. 2016. Beyond Affordable Housing: Whither Community Land Trust? (Unpublished master thesis). Tufts University, Massachusetts, MA. Retrieved from *https:// search.proquest.com/docview/1845020646/abstract/403E6A87BB5F42C7PQ/1.* Accessed 20 August 2019.

Walker, A. P. P. (2016). Self-help or public housing? Lessons from co-managed slum upgrading via participatory budget. *Habitat International, 55*, 58–66. *https://doi.org/10.1016/j.habitatint.2016.02.005.*

Ward, P. M. (1989). Land values and valorization processes in Latin American cities: a research agenda. *Bulletin of Latin American Research, 8*(1), 47–66. *https://doi.org/10.2307/3338893.*

Watson, V. (2009). Seeing from the South: Refocusing urban planning on the globe's central urban issues. *Urban Studies, 46*(11), 2259–2275. *https://doi.org/10.1177/0042098009342598.*

Wekesa, B. W., Steyn, G. S., & Otieno, F. A. O. (2010). The response of common building construction technologies to the urban poor and their environment. *Building and Environment, 45*(10), 2327–2335. *https://doi.org/10.1016/j.buildenv.2010.04.019.*

Werlin, H. (1999). The slum upgrading myth. *Urban Studies, 36*(9), 1523–1534. *https://doi.org/10.1080/0042098992908.*

Williamson, T. (2018, July). Community Land Trusts in Rio's Favelas. *Land Lines.* Retrieved from *https://www.lincolninst.edu/publications/articles/community-land-trusts-rios-favelas.* Accessed 5 August 2019.

Williamson, T. (2019). *The Favela Community Land Trust: A Sustainable Housing Model for the Global South.* In A. Fitz, E. Krasny, & A. Wien (Eds.), Critical Care: Architecture and Urbanism for a Broken Planet. MIT Press.

World Habitat. n.d. "World Habitat Awards: Caño Martín Peña Community Land Trust." *World Habitat.* Retrieved from *https://www.world-habitat.org/world-habitat-awards/winners-and-finalists/cano-martin-pena-community-land-trust/.* Accessed 13 August 2019.

Yahya, S. S. (2002). Community Land Trusts and other tenure innovations in Kenya. In *Land, Rights & Innovation: Improving Tenure Security for the Urban Poor* (pp. 233–263). Practical Action Publishing.

Zonta, M. (2016). Community Land Trusts: A Promising Tool for Expanding and Protecting Affordable Housing. *Center for American Progress.* Retrieved from *https://cdn.americanprogress.org/wp-content/uploads/2016/06/14141430/CommunityLandTrusts-report.pdf.* Accessed 20 August 2019.

2.

Seeding the CLT in
Latin America and the Caribbean

Origins, Achievements, and the
Proof-of-Concept Example of the
Caño Martín Peña Community Land Trust

*María E. Hernández-Torrales, Lyvia Rodríguez Del Valle,
Line Algoed, and Karla Torres Sueiro*

The Fideicomiso de la Tierra del Caño Martín Peña (Caño CLT) is a community land trust designed and controlled by the residents of seven neighborhoods along the Martín Peña Channel, a highly polluted tidal estuary that runs through the heart of San Juan, the capital of Puerto Rico. The Caño CLT was created with the aim to regularize land tenure and to prevent involuntary displacement and gentrification, precipitated by the government's planned dredging and clean-up of the channel. Creation of the Caño CLT and the channel's ecological restoration are among the main elements of the wider ENLACE Caño Martín Peña Project. This initiative has brought together community residents and partners from the private and public sectors to implement a comprehensive development plan designed to uplift a historically marginalized area, while transforming this urban area into a more habitable, just and participatory space.

Residents of seven Martín Peña neighborhoods[1] adopted the community land trust (CLT), but adapted it to meet local needs. By adding completely new elements to the model and by applying it to address the problem of land insecurity in an informal settlement, the Caño CLT has become an important reference world-wide, specifically in the Global South. Roughly 1,500 very low- to moderate-income households are now members of the Caño CLT, which currently owns and manages more than 110 hectares (272 acres) of land, most of which previously belonged to governmental agencies. The Caño CLT ensures the availability of permanently affordable housing and provides alternative housing options on its land for families who have had to relocate because of the dredging of the channel. It is also an instrument for the generation and redistribution of wealth.

The Fideicomiso de la Tierra del Caño Martín Peña is one of three institutions that resulted from a broad participatory planning-action-reflection process that took place between 2002 and 2004. During the planning process, twelve community-based organizations from the Martín Peña communities came together as a collective in the Group of the Eight Communities Adjacent to the Caño Martín Peña, Inc. (G-8). In collaboration with external partners from Puerto Rico's private and public universities and other professional and technical allies, they drafted regulatory instruments such as the Comprehensive Development and Land Use Plan for the Special Planning District of the Caño Martín Peña (the District Plan) and Law 489 of September 24, 2004 for the Comprehensive Development of the Special Planning District of the Caño Martín Peña (Law 489-2004). Through this law, not only the Caño CLT was created, but also a government corporation, the ENLACE Project Corporation, charged with responsibility for implementing the District Plan with a prominent role of the residents.

Initially conceived to regularize land tenure, to facilitate the implementation of the District Plan and to guarantee access of these consolidated communities to urban land whose value was increasing, the Caño CLT is continuing its work in the midst of a double crisis. Puerto Rico has been struggling with financial distress and an unpayable public debt since 2006. Then, two devastating hurricanes hit the island in September 2017.[2] Puerto Rico has become one of the only places in the world that is simultaneously going through the contradictory processes of both austerity and recovery, while exhibiting the designs and dangers of what is known as "disaster capitalism" (Bonilla & LeBron, 2019; Algoed & Hernández, 2019).

Puerto Rico is an unincorporated territory of the United States, a result of the Cuban-Spanish-American War when the United States installed colonial governments in the Philippines, Guam and Puerto Rico. Today, Puerto Rico and Guam continue to be under U.S. sovereignty. According to the U.S. Census Bureau, in 2018 Puerto Rico had a population of 3.2 million. Since the start of the financial crisis, however, half-a-million Puerto Ricans have left the island. Another 160,000 emigrated to the United States after Hurricane María.[3] When the Caño CLT was created, the main threats faced by the communities along the channel were involuntary displacement and gentrification, a result of an increase in the value of the area's land. Today, the main threat comes from a decrease in value which, in combination with the government's current austerity and disaster recovery policies, have created conditions favorable to speculation. Under both cycles of increasing and decreasing land value, the Caño CLT has proven to be an effective instrument to protect the community against displacement.

This chapter discusses how the Caño CLT is facilitating the regularization of land tenure in seven informal settlements, while preventing gentrification and furthering implementation of the District Plan. Inhabitants of this area transformed an infrastructure project that was initially led by the government into a participatory project of comprehensive development, one that is working to overcome historical causes of poverty, while also restructuring the government's relationship with the marginalized communities within this special planning district. Together with their external partners, the Caño residents have created a viable CLT that aims to protect their right to land, their right to adequate housing, their right to live in the city with dignity, their right to health, and their right to participate in the decisions that affect their future, including those related to the use and development of their land. The components of this project combine to counteract the way in which a lack of community participation in large-scale infrastructure projects normally leads to forced displacement and structural urban inequality.

The ability of G-8, ENLACE, and the Fideicomiso de la Tierra to unite people toward a common cause in a deeply divisive context has been recognized internationally. Since winning the United Nations World Habitat Award in 2016, the Caño CLT has become an example and an inspiration for activists around the world who are working on land tenure issues and looking for an alternative form of land regularization. One of only two communities land trusts in the world that have been organized in an informal settlement,[4] the Caño CLT has become a touchstone for communities in the Global South in particular, who are looking to establish CLTs of their own to overcome the threat of displacement from lands strategically located in desirable areas.

The chapter is organized into four sections. First, we present a historical overview and political context to help the reader to understand that, although Puerto Rico is part of the United States, the multiple obstacles faced by the Martín Peña communities are both enormous and exceptional. Then, we describe how the Caño CLT was created and why the communities opted for a CLT to address their needs. After explaining how the CLT functions, we reflect on the importance of the Fideicomiso as a reference for other communities that are struggling with similar threats of displacement from their land and why they might look to the Caño CLT for inspiration.

I. LAND, DISPLACEMENT AND INFORMAL SETTLEMENTS IN PUERTO RICO

The relationship with the land has always been a subject of struggle in Puerto Rico. As in the rest of Latin America, the history of Puerto Rico is defined by colonialism and the repeated displacement of vulnerable populations. A colony of the United States since 1898, the Caribbean island lacks economic sovereignty. Decades of dependence and tax exemptions aimed at attracting and extracting wealth have put major stresses on the island's economy. With a current unaudited public debt of over $74 billion, the Commonwealth of Puerto Rico was forced to apply austerity measures, imposed by the Fiscal Oversight Board created under PROMESA (Puerto Rico Oversight, Management and Economic Stability Act). This law, adopted by the U.S. Congress in 2016 during the Obama presidency, created the Fiscal Oversight Board to guarantee payments to bondholders, most

> Little by little, control of the island's land has moved to those who do not use it for the benefit of the country.

of them speculators. Public employees and retirees have been seeing their salaries and pensions jeopardized, approximately 280 schools have been closed, and the budget of the public university has been drastically reduced. Insecurity due to the cuts, the high unemployment rate, and the high cost of living have made life on the island challenging for a large part of its population.

This economic crisis is the result of the expiration of federal tax exemptions for United States companies, which had previously turned the island into one of the more attractive places to locate for North American companies. The growth of the economy depended on these tax exemptions. When these tax exemptions expired in 2006, most of the companies abandoned Puerto Rico, leaving thousands of highly skilled Puerto Ricans unemployed. There has been virtually no economic growth since then.

Land is one of the only assets that the government can still monetize. Tax incentives that took place after 2012 have attracted investors to the island to buy land to develop luxury complexes. Little by little, control of the island's land has moved to those who do not use it for the benefit of the country, during a period when it has become increasingly difficult for Puerto Ricans to find employment, to buy land, or to pay off their mortgage loans. Disaster recovery and other policies adopted after Hurricanes Irma and María have exacerbated the situation. Puerto Rico is almost fully under the Opportunity Zones program, which provides generous U.S. federal tax exemptions to investors and is particularly attractive for the real estate sector. Meanwhile, the Action Plan[5] prepared by Puerto Rico and approved by the U.S. Department of Housing and Urban Development has a series of policies that promote the displacement of communities in high-risk areas, even when mitigation is feasible. Concurrently, the government permits privately funded reconstruction and developments in similar high-risk areas.

Investing in luxury properties in depressed sectors — which, in the case of Puerto Rico, includes most of the island — can result in increases in the land values, contributing to the displacement of low-income and moderate-income residents. The displacement of poor communities can, in turn, lead to further increases in land values (Navas, 2004: 4).

According to the government Office for Socio-Economic and Community Development, there are 742 communities across Puerto Rico that have been categorized as informal settlements. The rapid industrialization of the island in the 1930s and 1940s, which made Puerto Rico an example of "advanced capitalism," pushed impoverished peasants into the coastal cities in search of employment and health and education services for their children. As affordable housing was not available, they occupied land that was unsuitable for housing, such as mangroves, wetlands, steep mountain slopes, and areas very close to the sea. Many of these families settled in the wetlands along the Martín Peña Channel, at the outskirts of San Juan, building makeshift homes on stilts with cardboard, coconut trees, wood, and tin. They used wooden planks to create connections among the homes

Fig. 2.1. Aerial view of neighborhoods surrounding the Martín Peña Channel (top), and a house alongside the Martín Peña Channel. LINE ALGOED / J.E. DAVIS

and to have access to the dry land and roads. With time, the families and the Municipality of San Juan filled the wetlands with debris.

Today, almost 25,000 people still live in eight neighborhoods along the channel. As the city grew, their location became prime real estate next to the financial district and along the channel that, once dredged, will serve as an inland waterway connecting the main airport with tourist-oriented hubs. The once-navigable channel is clogged and heavily polluted, as most neighborhoods lack an adequate sewage system and functioning storm-water management systems.

Between the 1960s and 1980s, as development policies were aimed at eliminating "slums," several communities along the western half of the Caño were relocated to

Fig. 2.2. One of the Caño's major streets, looking toward San Juan's financial district (top) and a side street in a Caño neighborhood. DOEL VÁZQUEZ / J.E. DAVIS

public housing or evicted. There were various proposals to recover the Caño area either for conservation purposes, for highways or for high-end developments including hotels and marinas. Most of these plans called for the displacement of remaining Martín Peña communities. Relocation costs were not even considered, and neither was community participation (Algoed, Hernández and Rodríguez, 2018). With the establishment of the financial district and the advancement of individual land-titling programs, gentrification became a new threat. Speculators started buying those individually owned plots of land, particularly those closest to the main transportation corridors, knowing that the possible ecosystem restoration of the channel would drastically increase the value of the area's land. These threats, coupled with the announcement in 2002 that the government was going to pursue the dredging of the channel, would become the issues around which the residents of the Martín Peña communities organized to find a solution for their common problems.

II. CREATION OF THE CAÑO MARTÍN PEÑA CLT

Public participation in the planning process for government-sponsored projects that affect residential areas has rarely happened in Puerto Rico. That remained the pattern even after the Puerto Rico Planning Board was mandated by law to open the planning processes to comments and participation by the public. This started to change under the administration of Governor Sila M. Calderón. In March 2001, the Governor signed the first statute of her new administration, proclaiming as a public policy the empowerment of residents of low-income communities (Law 1, March 1, 2001). This public policy encouraged citizen partic-ipation, defined as a comprehensive process enabling citizens to recognize and to exercise full control of their lives, starting from their own efforts and power. According to the Law, such an initiative would be aimed at helping the residents of low-income communities to acquire the skills and levels of organization that might allow them to become authors of their own process of economic and social development. The government would act as a train-er, promoter, facilitator, and collaborator, eliminating barriers and creating the necessary conditions and mechanisms to enable communities to secure their personal and commu-nity development. Governmental agencies and instrumentalities were required to carry out well-planned actions to stimulate the participation of low-income communities in the deci-sion-making processes related to the issues affecting their development. These communities would assume new roles as owners and producers, implementing a participatory approach to planning and improving their neighborhoods, which was radically different from the past practice of being passive beneficiaries of a paternalistic state. This public policy enabled the participatory approach that was used in the ENLACE Project.

From an Infrastructure Project
to a Sustainable Development Project

Instead of hiring engineers, the Authority hired an urban planner to lead the effort and estab-lished a Community Participation Office in a trailer located at the heart of the Caño com-munities, and staffed with community social workers and organizers. The Authority also pursued the establishment, by the Puerto Rico Planning Board, of the Caño Martín Peña Special Planning District, comprised by seven of the eight communities[6] remaining along the tidal channel. Residents participated in high numbers during the first round of commu-nity assemblies as they learned about the plans to dredge the channel, and strongly voiced their concern around displacement. They questioned where the families living close to the channel would be taken, as the space was needed for the dredging. Moreover, and conscious of the strategic location of their neighborhoods, they questioned who would benefit from the project, and clearly expressed their intent to oppose any attempt to gentrify. The meeting

Fig. 2.3. Election of new community council for Comunidad Las Monjas, one of the Caño's G-8 communities. LINE ALGOED

sparked one of the most successful participatory community development processes in Puerto Rico's history.

From 2002 to 2004, more than 700 participatory planning, action, and reflection activities were held in the Martín Peña communities. Concurrently, residents were envisioning the future and designing strategies, implementing projects and programs for short-term wins addressing their pressing issues, while organizing and critically thinking and learning about the process that was being implemented. The residents received the information they needed to participate intelligently in drafting the development plan, and technical consultants engaged in a dialogue that valued the knowledge of the residents rather than downplaying it. Had residents been left out of this process, the plan would have been inadequate and incomplete. The end result was the *Comprehensive Development and Land Use Plan for the Caño Martín Peña Special Planning District* (Development Plan), which was officially adopted by the Puerto Rico Planning Board and approved by the Governor of Puerto Rico in 2007. The inclusive process that produced this Plan took what had started out as a typical top-down engineering project and turned it the participatory, equitable and sustainable community development initiative called the ENLACE Caño Martín Peña Project.

Today, there are approximately 120 community leaders active within the G-8, mostly women and youth; indeed, 40% are young leaders between the ages of 11–25 years old. Another 100 residents form a network with a person per-street who is tasked with keeping their neighbors informed of the activities that are taking place, as thirty different socio-economic, housing, and urban development initiatives are underway with residents playing an active role in each.

Development Without Displacement

The Development Plan assumed that the Martín Peña communities would gain control over the publicly owned land within the Caño Martín Peña Special Planning District. This would accomplish three important goals. First, land would become available for the housing and infrastructure projects necessary to improve the quality of life of the residents and to address constant flooding with polluted water. Taking the cost of land out of the equation, moreover, would lower the implementation costs and increase the project's feasibility in the context of Puerto Rico's dire financial and economic situation. Second, having control of the land would allow residents who were living in areas where land was needed to build infrastructure projects and to dredge the channel to be relocated within one of the Caño's neighborhoods, avoiding their involuntary displacement. Third, gentrification would be prevented. Community residents were aware that once the infrastructure project took place and the channel was dredged, the cost of land and housing within the Martín Peña area would soar and existing residents would surely and steadily be pushed aside. With this in mind, having control of the land would prevent the displacement of residents who lacked land titles by regularizing their relationship with the land and allowing them to have security of tenure.

> Residents were aware that once the channel was dredged, the cost of land would soar.

Land ownership was a central piece for the community to reach its goal, so choosing the right mechanism to regularize tenure was critical. Several strategies were used to provoke discussions around land tenure. To help with the anaylsis of tenure options, a Housing Committee was created, composed of representatives from the seven Caño neighborhoods in the Special Planning District.

A workshop was held where participants were asked to identify why families wanted to have individual titles to the land — the form of tenure with which people were most familiar. The common answers included: the desire of the residents to bequeath the right to occupy a parcel of land to their legal heirs; access to public services (i.e., safe connections to the power grid required a permit); and access to mortgage credit. All participants agreed that avoiding the displacement of the community was a priority. After learning from experts about the pros and cons of individual land titles, land coops, and community land trusts, participants were able to examine how each ownership instrument might allow them to reach their objectives. The workshop opened the participants' eyes to the possibility of considering a broader range of options, beyond the one with which they were most familiar. The discussion continued in community assemblies, including one in which a Spanish-speaking member of the Dudley Street Neighborhood Initiative in Boston shared their experiences.

Deliberations of the Housing Committee were rooted in six critical rights that were deemed to be indispensable for any instrument they might choose for controlling land, including:

- the right to stay put;

- the right to land tenure;

- the right to adequate housing;

- the right to property for individual residents;

- the right to benefit from improvements to the area; and

- the right to participate in the decision-making process and implementation of the District Plan.

Residents made a conscientious and audacious decision. They concluded that some form of collective land ownership was the only way to prevent gentrification and, despite the absence of any other CLT in Puerto Rico at the time, they concluded that a CLT would be the best option for enabling the Martín Peña communities to have control of the land. A community land trust would make possible the dredging of the Martín Peña Channel, the construction of needed infrastructure, and the rehabilitation of their neighborhoods, just as residents had envisioned in the Development Plan. The land was to be collectively owned in perpetuity, while each family who formerly lacked a land title would obtain a legal document — a surface rights deed — that would secure their right to use the land beneath their home, a right they would be able to bequeath to their legal heirs. This deed would enable them to stay put and to have a livelihood in the city, while securing their right to influence what might happen in their own neighborhood. They would no longer have to fear speculators, nor gentrification and involuntary displacement. With this decision behind them, they proceeded to secure the land and to initiate a new two-year participatory process to design how the first community land trust in Puerto Rico would manage its assets.

> They would no longer have to fear speculators, nor gentrification and involuntary displacement.

III. STRUCTURE AND FUNCTION OF THE CAÑO CLT

The Fideicomiso de la Tierra del Caño Martín Peña is a community land trust, constituted as a private, nonprofit organization created in perpetuity with an independent juridical identity. The Caño CLT is authorized to acquire land within and outside the Special Planning District, to develop and to sell housing (and other buildings), and to re-acquire these structural improvements, exercising a right of first refusal whenever owners desire to sell. The Caño CLT is entitled to create strategies and to design resale formulas which ensure the affordability of housing in perpetuity.

The CLT is a membership organization with an eleven-member Board of Trustees that is composed of community, private and government representatives, as follows: four

Trustees are Caño CLT members, whose homes are located on the lands owned by the Caño CLT; two Trustees are residents of the Martín Peña communities, designated to serve on the CLT's Board by the G-8; two Trustees are non-residents of the District, selected by the Board's members, based on skills and knowledge they can contribute to the CLT. The three remaining spaces are occupied by representatives of governmental entities, one from the Corporación del Proyecto ENLACE Board of Directors, one from the San Juan Municipality designated by the city's mayor, and one selected by the Governor of Puerto Rico.[7]

Caño CLT General Regulations

The legal grounds for the *Reglamento General para el Funcionamiento del Fideicomiso de la Tierra del Caño Martín Peña*, Rule 7587 (hereafter Caño CLT General Regulations), are the Puerto Rico Law No. 489, September 24, 2004, known as *"Ley para el Desarrollo Integral del Distrito de Planificación Especial del Caño Martín Peña"* (Law 489-2004), and the Puerto Rico Administrative Procedures Law. Through a democratic and participative process, a community committee was organized during 2006–2008. This committee gathered representatives from all seven communities who participated in several activities and workshops in order to establish the basis for the Caño CLT's General Regulations in accordance to the needs and concerns of Martín Peña communities' residents. The Caño CLT General Regulations were adopted on October 8, 2008, setting the regulations for the governance and operation of the Caño CLT and the rules and procedures for guaranteeing the administration of the land in favor of the communities' residents.

Law 489-2004 entrusted the Proyecto ENLACE Corporation with the constitution and promulgation of the Caño CLT's regulations. Law 489-2004 also defined the basic processes through which land would be identified and entitled to become part of the Caño CLT and established the framework for the Caño CLT to assign members to its Board of Trustees (23 L.P.R.A. section 5048).

The Caño CLT's General Regulations consist of fourteen articles which regulate the administrative aspects and the operational processes of the Caño CLT.[8] They define the organization's mission, vision, goals and objectives; the land trust's assets; the criteria to qualify as a member of the CLT; the rights of membership; the collaborative arrangements with ENLACE Corporation and the G-8; and other obligations and powers of the Caño CLT. Also, the Caño CLT's General Regulations carefully ensure community participation in all governing bodies within the project and decision-making processes. In order to ensure such participation, a Registry of Members is used to notify and summon Caño CLT members for activities such as assemblies, elections, and other deliberations, all convened after timely notification. The General Regulations also set standards and procedures for convening assemblies, establishing a quorum, and making announcements.

The Proyecto ENLACE Corporation, which was also created by Law 489-2004, is a governmental corporation created with a sunset provision. It is charged with the responsibility to advance the implementation of the Development Plan. The ENLACE Corporation and the Caño CLT converge in a multidisciplinary and multifaceted project called Proyecto ENLACE. These entities play complementary roles in achieving the goals of Proyecto ENLACE. The relations and interactions between them are established in the General Regulations, including how they work together to identify plots of land in the District, to plan new developments, and to allocate economic and human resources to achieve common goals essential to advance Proyecto ENLACE. Standards and procedures to address and review short- and long-term strategic plans and priorities for housing allocation are also delimited.

Aims and Objectives of the Caño CLT

The Fideicomiso de la Tierra del Caño Martín Peña was created to safeguard the land tenure and residential permanence of residents living in the seven neighborhoods along the Martín Peña Channel, while allowing and promoting development within the District. Among others, the aims and objectives of the Caño CLT were specified in Law 489-2004 as follows:

- Contribute toward the solution of lack of ownership rights of many Special Planning District's residents through collective title landholding;

- Address with equity the physical or economic displacement of low-income residents arising from gentrification, avoiding displacement and eradication of the communities;

- Guarantee affordable housing within the Special Planning District;

- Acquire and administer lands on behalf of and in the best interest of the community, increasing local control over the land, and avoiding absentee owner decision-making; and

- Enable the reconstruction and valuation of urban spaces.

Law 489-2004, and other regulations adopted in accordance to this Law, vested the Caño CLT with the authority and powers to accomplish these objectives.

Transferring Public Land to the Caño CLT

Following its participatory planning-action-reflection process, the community decided to adopt the community land trust ownership structure for addressing the lack of legal title among hundreds of families living on both sides of the Martín Peña Channel, families whose homes were located on public lands. This publicly owned land was to be transferred to the Caño CLT, all of which would be permanently owned and managed by the Caño CLT. Rights to individual parcels within the Caño CLT's landholdings would be conveyed to the families who were already living there through a durable surface rights deed for each parcel. These transfers and tenures united elements of Puerto Rico Civil Law and United States Common Law. This arrangement also incorporated the definition of the community land trust model found in amendments to the National Affordable Housing Act, passed by the U.S. Congress in 1992.

Elements taken from a civil trust model were the basis for transferring the public land to an entity controlled by the residents of the communities along the Martín Peña Channel through the Caño CLT. This transfer was constituted by the following components:

- The *settlor* who transfers the land, which in this particular case was the government of Puerto Rico;

- The *trustee* who receives ownership of the land with responsibility for possessing and administering it for the benefit of the communities, which in this particular case was the Caño CLT; and

- The *beneficiaries* who benefit from the administration of the land, which in this particular case were the residents who owned a structure on a portion of the land that was transferred to the Caño CLT.

Law 489-2004, Article 22, establishes that the corpus of the Caño Martín Peña CLT is comprised of all the lands transferred to the ENLACE Corporation for the purpose of creating the Caño CLT, as well as those acquired in the future in accordance with Law 489-2004. In addition, the Caño CLT was required to be governed according to the CLT General Regulations referenced above. Creation of such regulations were entrusted to the ENLACE Corporation.

The Caño CLT has an express limitation under Law 489-2004, forbidding the CLT from selling the public lands that were transferred to it. The Caño CLT is required by law to retain permanent ownership of the land. The Caño CLT is able to sell or to transfer rights over the edifices that are built on the land, however, and is also authorized to grant surface rights deeds and long-term leases, subject to hereditary rights. Homeowners who live on the once-public lands that were conveyed to the Caño CLT individually own their buildings, but they do not own the underlying land. The land is owned and managed by the Caño CLT for the common benefit of the Martín Peña communities, present and future.

Surface Rights Deeds

The transfer of public lands to the Caño CLT was mandated by Law 489-2004.[9] A majority of the government agencies that owned and controlled these lands at the time could not provide official documentation identifying the land registrar information, however; nor was there an official record of boundaries and value, making it difficult to proceed with transferring these public lands. This situation slowed down the work plan of the ENLACE Corporation.[10] To get a jump-start, volunteers for the Caño CLT made good efforts and identified registry information for some of the biggest parcels of land. Accordingly, a deed was authorized, specifying registry data for such properties.

The process of identifying and acquiring land is continuous, as the Caño CLT is constantly undergoing title investigations to identify parcels of land that may be transferred into its ownership. Currently, the Caño CLT owns and administers just over 110 hectares (272 acres) of land. Most of it (200 acres) was part of the original transfer of publicly owned land under Law 489-2004; another part of the CLT's landholdings (72 acres) was added gradually over the years as ENLACE acquired privately owned houses (with title to the land) to relocate homeowners directly impacted by the canal's dredging and then conveyed those parcels to the CLT.[11] All of this land, which is scattered throughout the seven neighborhoods of the Caño Martín Peña Special Planning District, is administered in the best interests of the Caño's residents, consistent with Law 489-2004, the District Plan, and the General Regulations.

One of the responsibilities of the Caño CLT is to identify those households who can benefit from a surface rights deed and to grant them such a deed in accordance with Law 489-2004. There are approximately 1,500 households living on the CLT's lands. To date, 110 surface rights deeds have been executed.[12] It is a slow and laborious process, since prior to executing the deed all documentation must be in place and the person or persons who appear on the deed must be the ones who have the legal right to do so.[13]

Through these surface rights deeds, the Caño CLT conveys individual property rights to those residents who own a housing structure on the Caño CLT's land. Homeowners possess the right to occupy and use the surface of the land beneath their homes, but they do not own the land itself. Generally, surface rights are granted in perpetuity or for a specific term. For its validity, surface rights are secured through public deeds that are then registered in the Puerto Rico Property Registry. After being officially registered, this legal instrument allows for two owners to co-exist in possessing separate portions of the same space: the Caño CLT owns the land and the resident owns the structure. The latter enjoys all the benefits of using, improving, and even mortgaging the surface right, as delimited by the Caño CLT in the surface rights deed.[14]

Fig. 2.4. Sixta Gladys Peña-Martínez, Caño CLT member and G-8 community leader, signing the surface rights deed for the land beneath her home, May 20, 2016.
MARÍA E. HERNÁNDEZ-TORRALES

Publicly registered surface rights deeds specify the footprint under a resident's home, delineating the portion of land for which the right is granted. These deeds also identify the rights and obligations of the person to whom the surface right was conferred. Contained in the public deed, there is also a description of the housing structure. This is a legal requirement that allows the registration of the housing structure as a unit separate from the land. Other contents included in the surface rights deed are designed to protect houses on the CLT's land from non-mortgage or non-governmental debt claims under Puerto Rico's Safe Home Act.

The surface right's value amounts to 25% of the value of the plot of land on which a resident's home is located, becoming straightaway an asset for a family and increasing their wealth.[15] Surface rights can be inherited and mortgaged. Families can sell their surface rights, but not the underlying land. The Caño CLT retains a first right of refusal to purchase both the house and the surface rights whenever a homeowner decides to sell. By these means, the Caño CLT permanently holds title to the land and permanently controls the future disposition of the buildings located thereon, managing these assets for the benefit of the Martín Peña communities and future generations.

To the best of our knowledge, the Caño CLT is the first community land trust that has been used for the relocation of families, allowing for the construction of public infrastructure and following the parameters of the federal Uniform Relocation Act. Using a transfer of rights mechanism, the relocation process cost is reduced. Families can trade the houses in which they have been living — which, in most cases, are deteriorated and likely located on plots of land to which the families do not have a right — in exchange for a new house in better conditions, joining the Caño CLT and enjoying surface rights. The Proyecto ENLACE Corporation is in charge of the process of acquiring and building homes and relocating families.

IV. THE POTENTIAL FOR WIDER USE OF CLTs IN INFORMAL SETTLEMENTS

As of 2016, it was estimated that approximately 54.5% of the world's population lives in urban settlements; 828 million of these urban dwellers live in densely populated informal settlements, characterized by the lack of land tenure, inadequate and unsafe infrastructure, and insufficient sanitary installations (UN-Habitat, 2013: 112). In Latin America and the Caribbean, approximately 113 million people live in informal settlements (UN-Habitat, 2013: 127).

After almost a century of marginalization, the residents of the neighborhoods along the Martín Peña Channel, who had lived and struggled for decades with the collateral damage of living in an informal settlement, organized to create the Fideicomiso de la Tierra del Caño Martín Peña that is now working to overcome infrastructural, residential, environmental, and socio-economic deprivations and inequalities that accumulated over many decades.

The Caño CLT is an innovative, effective, and empowering organization that may serve as an example for other informal settlements around the world. Its potential for inspiring and informing land rights struggles in other countries was the reason for the

Caño CLT being internationally recognized by World Habitat in 2016. Since receiving a World Habitat Award, members of the Caño CLT have been widely sharing their experiences and instruments with community leaders in informal settlements in Latin American, the Caribbean, and South Asia, encouraging them to adapt the practices pioneered in San Juan to their own needs and contexts, possibly using a CLT to enable residents to gain secure use of land, to stop displacements, and to take control of local development.

Communities that are the most similar to the Martín Peña communities — and that have the greatest potential for adopting and adapting a Fideicomiso de la Tierra — are those that exhibit the following characteristics:

* A significant number of residents live on lands to which they do not have a valid or legal title for lands that may be owned by the government, by private individuals, or by a corporation. Alternatively, these lands may be occupied and used under some form of communal landholding system that has yet to be recognized and registered by the state.

* There are mechanisms available to acquire the land, including donation, adverse possession, purchase, or intervention by the state;

* A significant percentage of the population has a high sense of community cohesion and belonging; and

* The informal settlement is located within an area — or proximate to one — where land values are rising or where lands are coveted by speculative investors, threatening the present population with displacement.

The following ingredients have been essential to the success of the Fideicomiso de la Tierra del Caño Martín Peña. They should be considered by other communities when contemplating, planning, or attempting to create a CLT of their own.

Holistic Approach

The Caño CLT is part of a broader plan that was designed using a participatory process. This plan presumed that community organizations and inter-sectoral alliances would both be involved in its implementation. The plan itself included a multi-faceted focus on environmental justice, personal health, violence prevention, food sovereignty, young leadership, a solidarity economy, educational transformation, adult literacy, equitable relocation, quality public spaces, a right to the city, and securing land tenure and affordable housing in perpetuity.

Community Organization and Democracy

A CLT should be designed and developed through democratic processes promoting citizen participation, where citizens are the ones who identify their needs and priorities and who make decisions about the best ways to address these needs. For a CLT to be effective, communities must take part in the planning process and adapt the CLT to their context, needs, and expectations. Organizing and participation must continue even after a CLT has been created. Residents who live on a CLT's land and around that land must have a sense of solidarity and tranquility that comes from being part of an organization that protects their homes and interests. When asked to describe in one word what the Caño CLT means to her, Margarita Cruz, a resident of the Las Monjas community, said "Us. We are the Fideicomiso". A goal of every CLT should be to foster such a sentiment.

Capacity Building, Leadership and Skills Development

Popular education is a significant tool to achieve effective participation of communities. Community leaders should facilitate and promote the participation of residents in the activities of the community and in the design of participative strategies, ensuring that the needs and concerns of residents are heard and considered. Participatory processes are continuous and require capacity building and spaces for constant reflection.

Alliances

Professional support is fundamental. A multidisciplinary team of social workers, planners, urbanists, lawyers, architects, engineers, artists, and many more must work together with communities to advance and to execute a holistic plan. This kind of multidisciplinary team must value community knowledge, must promote critical thought, organization, and the exchange of knowledge between residents and professionals, and must stimulate alternate visions to understand local realities. By observing attentively and listening respectfully, outside professionals can respond to the community's agenda.

Multi-sectoral Associations

Community projects need the support of private and public sectors and academics in order to succeed. These associations expand the exposure of a community's struggles, giving more visibility, while also contributing technical knowledge and resources.

Legal Framework

It is necessary to pay close attention to the legal framework for the ownership and management of land, even if it means a community must create new instruments. Residents of the communities along the Martín Peña Channel examined different forms of land tenure, evaluating individual and collective options for owning the land. They decided on a community land trust, an innovative form of tenure never before used in Puerto Rico. Thereafter, new legislation was promoted in order to establish the Fideicomiso de la Tierra del Caño Martín Peña. The creation of Law 489 in 2004 was the result of an extensive dialogue among many knowledgeable people, but it was also the consequence of an intense political process.

Solidarity with Communities in
Other Countries Facing Similar Challenges

With the aim of sharing the strategies and instruments developed by residents of the Caño Martín Peña with other communities around the world, the Caño CLT is working on a new initiative called the "Espacio de Encuentro Internacional del Fideicomiso de la Tierra." This initiative will facilitate dialogue among community leaders, activists, academics, and politicians from countries and cities in the Caribbean, Latin America, Asia, Africa, North America, and Europe on collective, cooperative, and community-controlled forms of land tenure in informal settlements. It will also serve as an educational center and monitoring network, aimed at producing new knowledge about the creation of community land trusts and the effective participation of community residents in the equitable development and inclusive improvement of informal settlements. Through this initiative, the Caño CLT is now developing the logistics to spread the tools and instruments of the Fideicomiso throughout Puerto Rico and globally.

The Caño CLT convened an international peer exchange on April 29–May 4, 2019 in San Juan. With the title "Community Development and Collective Land Ownership," the Caño CLT gathered community members and residents from informal settlements around the world who are threatened with displacement or who anticipate such a threat in the near future. Community leaders from Argentina, Barbuda, Brazil, Belize, Bolivia, Chile, Ecuador, Jamaica, Mexico, Bangladesh and South Africa traveled to Puerto Rico. In every case, there was a representative from a community-based organization and/or from other allies who could support the development and organization of a CLT in their communities once they returned to their countries of origin.[16]

Participants shared experiences from their own communities and organizations. Many of their stories mirrored the experience of the Martín Peña communities, as participants reflected on the relevance of the Caño's struggle and trajectory for their own realities, identifying common factors in the struggles they face and finding similarities in their own journeys. They saw they have many things in common, even when they are from different countries. Strong bonds were established, based on similarity and solidarity. During the peer exchange and in feedback provided at the end, participants expressed how important it was to gather together and to realize that people are struggling with similar issues all around the world. They are not alone. They are stronger together.[17] It became clear that community organizing that provokes critical thinking and participation is central to addressing land tenure issues, particularly under a collective ownership regime.

CONCLUSION

A majority of CLTs in other countries have been established on lands that were vacant when acquired, allowing the construction of new homes; or CLTs have acquired vacant buildings and rehabilitated them. In both cases, these newly developed homes have been made available to a new group of low-income renters or homeowners. The Fideicomiso de la Tierra del Caño Martín Peña is different. It was created on lands where the homes of hundreds of families were already in existence and already occupied prior to creation of the CLT. "This CLT was born big," as residents often say.

The CLT developed by residents living in the seven Martín Peña communities provides a "proof of concept," demonstrating that CLTs can be an effective tool for regularizing land tenure in informal settlements threatened by displacement. A CLT can also provide for the redistribution of wealth and allow its members to gain control over a settlement's land, increasing their collective power.

The Caño CLT was developed by communities that experienced displacement firsthand, either by direct state action or by gentrification processes. It was designed to ensure that the much-needed environmental rehabilitation of the Caño did not result in the disappearance of the communities through increases in the value of the area's land. It was also born out of an aspiration for justice and equity, so that long-neglected communities and their residents would be the ones to benefit from a large-scale project they had long dreamed of, a project with the potential to transform both their neighborhood and the city.

Fig. 2.5. Mural in one of the Caño's neighborhoods, which reads: ". . . and for the first time we residents are creators of our own future." LINE ALGOED

As one of the late community leaders of the G-8, Mrs. Juanita Otero Barbosa, has said: "The Fideicomiso is the only salvation we have of continuing to exist and living in this community, so that they do not take us out of here" (Carrasquillo et al., 2009). In the current context, as the value of real estate in Puerto Rico is decreasing and as opportunities are soaring for speculation by outside investors who are buying up prime real estate all across the island, the Caño CLT has become increasingly relevant for the Martín Peña communities. Lands that used to belong to the government now belong collectively to the residents through the Caño CLT. These lands have been permanently removed from the market. There is no longer a risk of the government someday selling the land underneath the Martín Peña communities in order to monetize its value. As residents from the Martín Peña communities can often be heard to say, with pride and tenacity: "This land is ours, and nobody can take it away from us."

Notes

1. The Caño communities are: Barrio Obrero, Barrio Obrero Marina, Buena Vista Santurce, Israel-Bitumul, Buena Vista Hato Rey, Las Monjas, and Parada 27.

2. Puerto Rico is an archipelago in the Caribbean Sea. Besides the main island of Puerto Rico, there are two other important islands, Vieques and Culebra, as well as other keys and islets. For the purpose of this essay, we will refer to all of Puerto Rico as an "island."

3. This emigration estimate comes from the Center for Puerto Rican Studies at Hunter, City University of New York.

4. The other is the Voi-Tanzania CLT in Kenya, the subject of Chapter 14 in the present volume.

5. The Action Plan guides the use of the Community Development Block Grant for Disaster Recovery (CDBG-DR) allocated to Puerto Rico to cover the unmet needs remaining after emergency assistance and to mitigate risks.

6. The Cantera Peninsula community was a pioneer in elaborating its own comprehensive development and land use plan, adopted by the Puerto Rico Planning Board in 1995. Badly hit by hurricane Hugo on September 18, 1989, the first major hurricane that struck Puerto Rico since 1932, and as the reconstruction process was underway, residents realized their neighborhood was to be displaced for high end development projects. After partnering with others and organizing, in 1992 the Puerto Rico Legislature enacted Law 20 to create a government corporation that would work along with the community residents to rehabilitate the impoverished sector. The Cantera Community is not part of the Caño CLT, but the community leaders are part of the G-8.

7. Reglamento General para el Funcionamiento del Fideicomiso de la Tierra 2008, Art. V, sec. 2 (Caño CLT General Regulations).

8. These "general regulations" function much like the articles and bylaws that legally constitute most nonprofit organizations in the United States.

9. There are about 188 hectares (466 acres) of land within the Caño Martín Peña Special Planning District, but only the publicly owned land would be transferred to the Caño CLT, on which about 1,500 households were already living.

10. It is important to note that almost half of the residents at the Martín Peña communities have individual land titles as a result of clientelist practices of politicians, both at the state and municipal level. This means there are many instances where, comparing two neighbors on the same street, one might have had a land title conveyed by the government at a $1.00 cost to acquire the land underneath his or her home, while the other neighbor would remain without a land title. This practice endured for more than 30 years.

11. Most of the households who needed to be relocated to make space for the dredging have chosen to become members of the CLT have been provided with a new house and a surface rights deed.

12. This means that, as of October 2019, another 1390 households who are members of the CLT and who are living on lands owned by the CLT, were still waiting to receive their surface rights deed.

13. During the five years since 2014, the Caño CLT has received pro bono assistance from civil law notaries for the execution of these surface rights deeds.

14. 30 L.P.R.A. sec 6261-6276.

15. For persons who already owned and occupied houses on publicly owned land at the time it was transferred to the CLT, the CLT's board of trustees decided to award them a 25% share of the market value of the land underlying their houses. Should they later want to sell, the CLT will pay them that 25% of the land value. In the future, if the CLT develops new houses on land that it owns, a different policy may be put in place for these homes.

16. The peer exchange was divided into two sessions: one for Spanish and Portuguese speakers, gathering together fifteen international participants and participants from two communities in Puerto Rico; the other was for English speakers, gathering together thirty-one community leaders and representatives of community-based organizations.

17. During the peer exchange, an international conference was also held that was open to the general public, entitled "Recovery, Land Tenure, and Displacement: Perspectives from Grassroots and Community development." The conference discussed recovery initiatives after Hurricane María, land tenure issues in a global and local context, and the effects of gentrification that lead to displacement. Approximately 136 people heard about the Fideicomiso de la Tierra, followed by a dialogue with grassroots leaders from South Africa, Barbuda, and Argentina who talked about informality and threats to their homes and neighborhoods.

References

Algoed, L. and M.E. Hernández (2019). "Vulnerabilization and Resistance in Informal Settlements in Puerto Rico: Lessons from the Caño Martín Peña Community Land Trust." *Radical Housing Journal,* Vol 1(1): 29-47.

Algoed, L., M.E. Hernández Torrales, and L. Rodríguez Del Valle (2018). "El Fideicomiso de la Tierra del Caño Martín Peña: Instrumento Notable de Regularización de Suelo en Asentamientos Informales," Working Paper. Cambridge: Lincoln Institute of Land Policy.

Bonilla, Y. and M. LeBron (2019). *Aftershocks of Disaster: Puerto Rico Before and After the Storm.* (Chicago: Haymarket Books).

Carrasquillo, J., A. Cotté, V. Carrasquillo, and M. S. Pagán (2008). *Fideicomiso de la Tierra: Experiencias en el Proceso de Creación.* Escuela Graduada de Trabajo Social Beatriz Lasalle, Universidad de Puerto Rico.

Navas Dávila, G. (2004). "Fideicomiso social de la Tierra." Trabajo preparado para el Dr. Fernando Fagundo, Secretario de Transportación y Obras Públicas del Estado Libre Asociado de Puerto Rico.

UN-Habitat (2013). *State of the World's Cities 2012/2013.* Available from: *https://sustainabledevelopment.un.org/content/documents/745habitat.pdf* [Accessed 14 August 2019.]

UN-Habitat (2012). *Estado de las ciudades en América Latina y el Caribe, Brasil.* See also *Urban Development and Energy Access in Informal Settlements. A Review for Latin America and Africa,* ResearchGate. Available from: *https://www.researchgate.net/publication/309273730_Urban_Development_and_Energy_Access_in_Informal_Settlements_A_Review_for_Latin_America_and_Africa* [Accessed 25 Jul, 2019.]

3.

Adapting Features of Puerto Rico's Caño Martín Peña CLT to Address Land Insecurity in the Favelas of Rio de Janeiro, Brazil

Tarcyla Fidalgo Ribeiro, Line Algoed,
María E. Hernández-Torrales, Lyvia Rodríguez Del Valle,
Alejandro Cotté Morales, and Theresa Williamson

This chapter is the result of a collaborative research project between a nongovernmental organization based in Rio de Janeiro, Catalytic Communities, and Latin America's first community land trust — one of the world's only CLTs in an informal settlement—the Fideicomiso de la Tierra del Caño Martín Peña in San Juan, Puerto Rico. The aim of the research project was to study the potential of CLT instruments and strategies developed by the communities along the Martín Peña channel as a way to tackle insecure tenure in Rio's favela communities.[1]

Based on this research, we present recommendations on essential lessons when considering the creation of a community land trust in informal settlements, such as those that exist in Puerto Rico, Brazil, and most countries in the Global South. For the purpose of this essay, we have defined "informal settlements" as those where settlers have self-built homes in communal areas, on land to which they lack legal ownership, and on which they continue to live.[2] Many of these settlements have existed for several generations. Over time, therefore, they may become *consolidated*, whereby the building stock, access to some services, community ties, and a way of life have become firmly established, even as the residents' tenure has remained precarious; that is, their legal right to occupy the land beneath their homes has remained "informal." Regularization becomes a primary objective in these cases, the process to legally secure the occupancy and use of the lands underlying an informal settlement.

In this chapter, we identify a set of conditions that we have concluded must be in place in an informal settlement before considering the creation of a CLT as a primary land tenure and regularization strategy. We also present an analysis of legal strategies that we deem necessary to implement CLTs, specifically in the favelas (the informal settlements) of Rio de Janeiro. Our hope is that this chapter can serve other communities, organizers, and professionals who are interested in understanding the process of establishing a community land trust in an informal settlement.

There are very special elements to take into account in the creation of CLTs in the Global South, specifically in the context of informal settlements. The challenges of establishing a CLT in an informal settlement are quite different from those that are faced by CLTs in North American, British, and European cities. In those cities, new homes are usually being developed by a CLT at great financial cost, either through construction or rehabilitation, and then marketed to prospective homebuyers or renters who choose whether they want to come and live in this newly created housing. Before moving in, they can weigh whether living on land that is owned by a CLT and whether purchasing homes with limits on equity at resale will be acceptable to them. In informal settlements, by contrast, residents may in effect already own their homes, which were built by themselves or by previous generations. They often feel a sense of ownership of the underlying land, even when lacking legal documentation of their right to that land. Residents may be reluctant to share control over the land with a new organizational entity under a form of tenure that is foreign to them.

The type of organization we will discuss and propose here is designed, in part, to address such reluctance. A CLT in Brazil, therefore, like the one in Puerto Rico, would have to be organized and directed by community residents themselves in order to be successful.

In informal settlements across Latin America, especially in Brazil, there is an urgency to finding new strategies for securing land tenure. About half of Brazil's territory is estimated to lack full property rights (Ministério das Cidades, 2019). The legal precariousness of land tenure in the favelas has allowed arbitrary evictions by governments, like the many evictions that preceded two international sports events in Rio: the 2014 World Cup and the 2016 Olympic Games. The precariousness of tenure has also served as an excuse for governments to neglect the development of local infrastructure and the provision of adequate public services. Security of tenure and the regularization of land rights in the favelas thus become essential for realization of the right to secure, fully serviced neighborhoods and the right to the city (Soares Gonçalves, 2009).

Land regularization programs that have emphasized individual titling, where deeds to lands that were once occupied informally are conveyed to individual occupants, have often increased the risk of involuntary displacements, a result of market pressures that intensify in the wake of the legalization of land tenure. Even where forced evictions are not being implemented or where governments have invested public resources in on-site rehabilitation and upgrading programs, centrally located favelas face gentrification. In

Fig. 3.1. Fogueteiro favela, Central Rio de Janeiro. CATALYTIC COMMUNITIES

Rio, during the pre-Olympic period, gentrification, locally called *remoção branca*, or "white eviction," was widely reported in the local and international press, and debated during community events.

It is thus time to expand the conversation around land tenure beyond the legal aspects of land titling, and move away from the emphasis on individual ownership as the strategy for land regularization in informal settlements. Individual ownership has not protected informal communities from involuntary displacement and gentrification. The strategy to regularize land tenure must not be framed solely on "legalizing" how each individual relates to the parcel of land they occupy. Rather, it should be chosen by the residents themselves as part of a participatory process that helps them to move towards their vision for the future of their community. Land titling should not be an end in itself, but rather an instrument to achieve both collective and individual objectives. Such a process implies that there are options beyond individual titles, and that such options should be evaluated by the residents in accordance with their own priorities. A participatory approach of planning – action – reflection becomes the key to addressing land tenure.

This chapter starts with an overview of the situation in Rio de Janeiro's favelas today, where land insecurity has led to threats of eviction and gentrification. We describe past and present policies of land regularization in Brazil, arguing that these policies have not been able to put an end to involuntary displacements, which is why looking at mechanisms and policies that favor community ownership of land is a matter of great urgency. We then focus on the Fideicomiso de la Tierra del Caño Martín Peña, describing how residents of the Caño communities came to the conclusion that a community land trust was the best strategy to protect lands they and their families have inhabited for almost a century.

Finally, drawing upon lessons and insights we have gained from peer-to-peer exchanges between community leaders and staff of the Caño CLT in Puerto Rico and community leaders and technical supporters in Brazil, we present the legal implications for the establishment of a CLT in Rio de Janeiro's favelas. We then provide an analysis of conditions that must be present to make organizing a CLT both possible and feasible and we offer recommendations for community leaders, organizers, and supportive professionals to consider when taking the first steps toward creation of a CLT in an informal settlement.

I. RIO'S FAVELAS: INSECURE HOMES ON INSECURE LAND

Rio de Janeiro today has over 1000 favela communities, ranging in size from a handful to over 200,000 residents. Over 24% of the city's population lives in favelas, which constitute the city's primary affordable housing stock. The first community to be called a "favela" is today known as Morro da Providência (Providence Hill). The community's founders were formerly enslaved Africans who were recruited to fight in the bloody war of Canudos in Brazil's arid Northeast. They had been promised land in Rio de Janeiro, the nation's capital at the time, as payment for their military service. When they arrived in Rio in late 1897, however, no land was made available, so they settled on a hillside between the city center and the port. They named the hill "Morro da Favela" (Favela Hill) after the robust, spiny and resilient *favela* bush that dotted the hillsides of Canudos. Eventually, all of Rio's informal settlements — including ones settled long before, such as the community of Horto (settled in the early 1800s, still standing and fighting eviction today) — became known as favelas.

There are a number of facts essential to understanding why, over 122 years after the first favela was settled, the potential for Favela CLTs is currently galvanizing local organizers. First is the *scale* of the challenge. Rio's 1000 favelas today house over 1.4 million people, the vast majority of whom have no legal title for the land they occupy.

Second is the role of *race.* Rio was the largest slave port in world history and received five times the number of enslaved Africans as the entire USA. Slavery also lasted in Brazil 60% longer. Free men, who had previously been enslaved, had served in the bloody Canudos battle on behalf of their adopted nation. Denied their promised compensation, they squatted on land, starting a favela next to Rio's Port. Across the city, hundreds of thousands of other descendants of enslaved people and rural migrants joined them over the following generations. As a result, today's racial maps of Rio show that black and

Fig. 3.2. Morro da Providência today, Rio's first favela. CATALYTIC COMMUNITIES

mixed-race Brazilians tend to live in favelas, particularly in distant ones, while white Brazilians live mostly in upscale and centrally located regions.

Third is the historical *longevity* of these informal settlements. Rio's favelas, on average, are not the precarious "shanties" or exodus-desiring "slums" they are depicted as being in the mainstream media. Rather, they are well-established communities with a long history and a strong local cultural production and community investment.[3]

Finally, it is necessary to understand the intentional *neglect* inflicted on these communities. After 120 years, favela neighborhoods continue to be underserviced, over-policed, and insecure in their tenure. Rio is not a city that is only now beginning to urbanize. This happened decades ago, providing ample time for quality upgrades which never materialized.

Favelas Today: Products of a Cycle of Legitimized Neglect

One might argue that, at the outset, the founding of an informal settlement constitutes a failure of government, especially the failure to produce affordable, livable housing and a supportive neighborhood environment. Once consolidated, however, the real failure is to deny communities recognition, preservation, and improvement on their historic investment. When residents value their community and identify their *permanence* in the territory as a primary goal, however — not to mention when they have established a solid stock of self-built housing and other community amenities — this is a clear sign of a consolidated community or one that is on the path to consolidation. At this point, public policy should focus on identifying such communities and working with residents to detect needs and provide the services they lack, along with preserving community-built assets. In self-built communities, only residents are capable of accurately identifying their assets and needs and how best to preserve them and to address them. Thus, the need for community control over development becomes increasingly critical and just.

This realization has been recent. It came over the past decade, after Rio de Janeiro was selected the host city for the 2014 World Cup and the 2016 Olympics. Prior to 2008, the city had experienced economic stagnation for thirty years, and it was often assumed that underinvestment was due to a lack of public funds. During the Olympic build-up, however, the government spent over US$20 billion on infrastructure and other public improvements in Rio. Promises that were made to the favelas fizzled — including the Morar Carioca program which was supposed to upgrade all favelas by 2020 (Osborne, 2013). Instead, 77,000 favela residents lost their homes to forced evictions (Children Win, 2016).

In a handful of other favelas, the government gave out land titles and invested in policing to bring down crime rates. It also invested in formalizing public services (water, electricity) and community businesses. Community moto-taxi stands and other informally operated businesses now had to be registered, with associated fees and taxes paid up. That was also the case of access to critical utilities. Not coincidentally, this happened in favelas located in the city's touristy South Zone where land values are highest, and where eviction is the most politically difficult. These communities consequently experienced the beginning processes of gentrification, with the cost of living increasing, property values skyrocketing, renters leaving, hotels and bar chains opening up, and some homeowners

Fig. 3.3. Vidigal favela, Rio's most notably gentrifying favela. FELIPE PAIVA

selling, unaware that the value of their homes was monetarily (and emotionally) much greater than what they ended up accepting (Timerman, 2013).

It was at this point, and with the added support of community and international media (which replaced previous dependence on local media monopolies), that the government's policy of neglect and exploitation became explicit. A public official, unaware of the implications of his own comments, noted in 2013 that, "Favelas in the South Zone were fine when they provided cheap labor nearby. Not anymore." Residents of favelas are meant to serve, in other words, not to be served, or so it seems. When they are no longer useful, they need to move. When their land becomes valuable, they need to move. Such is the logic that permeates public policy and social relations across Rio's territory.

Favela organizers today are much more aware that what they are now experiencing and have always known is a vicious cycle of legitimized neglect. This has been the default policy of municipal and state governments toward favelas over generations. Lack of investment in the triad of services most-needed by communities (health, education, and sanitation) produces lack of opportunity and marginalization by the wider society, which in turn propels some residents toward criminal activity. This also makes favelas easy targets for criminal activity. When neighborhoods become known for crime, officials further justify their repressive actions, neglect, and evictions. And the cycle continues.

Despite this cycle, however, residents have built many resilient and culturally vibrant communities with immense potential. In Rio, favelas are also generally well-located across the urban fabric, most having been founded due to nearby employment and services. It is this patrimony they seek to defend and to build upon when residents insist that they want to remain in their neighborhoods. And this is why a tension surfaced during the pre-Olympic period: at the same time as communities facing eviction were being denied the titles they desired, communities facing gentrification spoke against individual titling. How could this be? Because titles, long thought to be a panacea, clearly didn't offer the type of protection that communities desired (Williamson, 2015).

Looking at land tenure alternatives is thus particularly urgent in the context of Rio de Janeiro. Instead of adopting mechanisms that offer the "right to speculate," favela organizers are searching for mechanisms that ensure the right to stay, along with greater access to public services, recognition of self-built community assets, and community control.

The Failure of Regularization Policies in Solving the Problem of Land Insecurity in Brazil's Favelas

More than fifty percent of Brazil's national territory is occupied in an informal or irregular way; that is, without formal title to the land. This started during Portuguese colonialism in the 16th Century. The change of this situation was only pursued in the 19th Century with enactment in 1850 of the Law of Lands.[4] Despite this legislative change, the scenario of uncontrolled land occupation continued, aggravated by a strong urbanization process that began in the 20th Century. Decades passed following passage of the Law of Lands, with no progress being made toward regularizing tenure in informal settlements. Nor were any new legislative or practical measures undertaken to solve the problem.

This scenario of neglect finally began to change in the urban context with the enactment of the Federal Constitution of 1988. It included a chapter dedicated to urban policy, the result of pressure applied by various social and technical movements in a struggle for urban reforms. This chapter of the Constitution would later be regulated by Federal Law 10.257 (2001), known as the City Statute, which introduced an important set of instruments for land regularization, providing a general guideline for national urban policy.

Despite growing attention to the problem of land insecurity in the form of legislation, land regularization as a public policy with wide-ranging pretensions was only instituted as a result of Law 11.977 (2009). This Law provided a basis for regularization of tenure that was focused on guaranteeing rights to the inhabitants of informal settlements and increasing the accountability of developers and real estate agents who contributed to the situation of land informality. The Law created a framework for land regularization, including provisions for the legal title and land registry for the lands occupied by residents of informal settlements. The Law also provided for territorial improvements and increased construction safety, and included measures aimed at improving social and economic conditions for residents of the country's favelas.

> Where land is most valuable, individual titling strengthens speculative investment.

Law 11.977 (2009) had little impact, however, because of its short duration. Its chapter on land regularization was revoked by Law 13.465 (2017), enacted after President Dilma Roussef was ousted from power. The new legislation altered the previous land regularization model, reducing it to a focus solely on the registration aspect; that is, the granting of title deeds to residents living in informal settlements. This Law emphasized individual titling through full private ownership, prioritizing registry regulation to the detriment of other dimensions of land regularization, especially those related to infrastructure improvements in the favelas and social assistance to residents, which had been essential components of the previous legislative framework, Law No. 11.977 (2009).

The most direct threat to the security of tenure came from the option given to the Brazilian legislature under this new law to distribute property titles to residents of informal settlements. In areas of the city where land is most valuable, individual titling strengthens speculative investment in real estate and increases the cost of living for the poorest residents. The increase in the cost of living is due to the introduction of (often exorbitant) fees for basic services such as water and electricity, the collection of property taxes, the forced formalization of local businesses, and the growth in new local businesses targeting a higher-income clientele. Meanwhile, the introduction of speculative development stimulates property sales by residents, which typically take place at values below the formal market rate, but above the values practiced in the informal market where properties were previously traded.

Nevertheless, like every policy intervention before it, this latest piece of legislation for land regularization has been marked by disputes and contradictions. Because it will fuel speculation, this new law directly threatens the security of tenure. It also denies the guarantee of low-income residents' right to services. On the other hand, this legal framework also makes it possible to mold a CLT, should full land rights be yielded to communities who want to create one. Careful monitoring of the implementation of this law is thus in order to ensure the security of the possession of the poorest.

II. ADAPTING INSTRUMENTS AND STRATEGIES OF THE CAÑO MARTÍN PEÑA CLT FOR POSSIBLE APPLICATION IN RIO'S FAVELAS

After ten years of work supporting hundreds of favela community organizers and then helping their communities to fight both government-sponsored evictions and market-led gentrification — one due to the absence of land titles and the other to their presence — Catalytic Communities (CatComm), a Rio de Janeiro-based nonprofit organization, began studying the potential of CLTs for Rio de Janeiro's favelas. In the early 2010s, the organization engaged with a number of academic and business partners who were familiar with the CLT model in the United States, theorizing and imagining its possible application to favelas. CLTs seemed to offer a solution that would support the residents of consolidated favelas in achieving their primary land security objective: *permanence*, the ability to stay put in neighborhoods where they are financially and emotionally invested, places where they feel a sense of belonging.

CLTs seemed to CatComm like they might be a good fit for formalizing Rio's favelas

Fig. 3.4. Asa Branca favela street life. CATALYTIC COMMUNITIES

because a CLT is organized and operated along the same lines as a favela: homes are built, bought, inherited, and sold on a parallel, affordable housing market, while the underlying land is seen as a common good. Meanwhile, residents work collectively to build and to maintain their community and to fight for improvements. Favelas are often on land that is publicly owned. These informal settlements are regarded as providing for the "social function" of land, as required by Brazil's Constitution. CLTs can guarantee the security of land tenure of vulnerable populations, while also retaining the non-monetary values that residents have often built in their communities. This is done through a flexible arrangement that is easily adapted to different local realities. But it is also an emancipatory arrangement, since all planning and management of the territory arises from the residents, who are now in a position to officially define development within their own territory.

Despite suspecting that CLTs might have potential for formalizing Rio's favelas, however, Catalytic Communities did not feel capable of introducing something so unfamiliar and theoretical into the public debate. The mental leap required to take a North American model in which CLTs are built from scratch, and applying it to decades-old informal settlements in Brazil, building demand (and power) in the favelas for adopting this model, seemed an impossibility.

It was in this context that CatComm learned of the Caño Martín Peña CLT in Puerto Rico. Not only did seven San Juan communities successfully make this mental leap, they also *realized* a vision of what informal settlements could achieve when building upon the basics of the North American CLT model and creating a CLT to fit their own circumstances. The Caño CLT had successfully demonstrated that establishing CLTs in Rio's favelas might be an effective strategy to halt forced evictions, while also addressing the challenges that typically come with individual land titles. These challenges include: higher costs of living, real estate speculation, and gentrification; individualistic thinking and the atomization of community; and a change in local culture due to the growth of *lógica mercadológica* (market-oriented logic), circumventing the traditional collective and demonetized exchanges on which favelas have historically been based. Community organizers in Rio's favelas typically spend so many years seeking individual titles as the primary solution to land insecurity that they rarely think about the brand-new set of challenges that await residents once those titles are issued. It is then too late to tackle these new challenges, since the mechanisms that might support resistance have by then been blunted through the introduction of the individualized logic of conventional titling.

> The CLT could function as an instrument of emancipation and empowerment.

The CLT, by contrast, seemed to offer a solution to *both* the first challenge (land security) *and* these secondary challenges. The CLT was not simply an arrangement for owning and managing land. As the Caño CLT had shown, it could also function as an instrument of emancipation and empowerment. The Caño CLT had demonstrated a growth in *unity* among seven neighborhoods as they participated in the community planning process that led to the establishment of their CLT, resulting in an incredibly rare level of *power* in their relationships with public authorities.

Caño Martín Peña CLT: Latin America's First CLT

For approximately 80 years, nearly 25,000 residents of the communities along the Caño Martín Peña (Martín Peña Channel) were invisible to government officials, at both the local and state levels. These communities, located in the heart of San Juan, Puerto Rico's capital city, were the result of rural migration during the economic crisis of the 1920s through the 1950s. Impoverished peasants moved with their families to the San Juan area looking for jobs and better living conditions. Most self-built their own housing. A number of families occupied dry land, but many built their homes on the wetlands along the Martín Peña Channel using cardboard, tin, and wood. A great number of them built their houses literally on the water. Over time the families and the municipal government filled the wetlands with all kinds of debris, creating dry land to sustain their makeshift homes. The city continued to grow, and soon the Caño communities found themselves in the heart of San Juan, next to its financial district. A place that no government administration wanted to look at or to care for became strategically located on valuable land that presented manifold development opportunities for the city and the country.

Government disinvestment and neglect, along with poor watershed management, led to a clogged channel. This was coupled with lack of adequate infrastructure, exposing residents of the Caño communities to an unhealthy environment. In 2002, however, after decades of studies and a lack of concrete action, the government announced its intention to dredge and to restore the Martín Peña Channel, reconnecting the lagoons, canals, wetlands, and beaches that are part of the San Juan Bay Estuary.

Having faced evictions and displacement in the past, residents of the Caño's communities inserted themselves into the planning process of what became the Caño Martín Peña Special Planning District in order to protect the permanence of their communities. They created the ENLACE Caño Martín Peña Project to spearhead the effort, completed with a strong community organizing and participation component.

Their participation turned an engineering project (unaware of its negative externalities) into a comprehensive development project (taking action to prevent such externalities) and led to the creation of public policy and institutions to make it feasible. Not only would the channel be cleaned and dredged, but improvements in stormwater and sewerage infrastructure were also planned in order to avoid further contamination, along with needed upgrades to the potable water and power infrastructure. It was recognized, too, that interventions would be needed to improve the quality of public spaces and inadequate housing, along with a sensible relocation strategy and socio-economic development initiatives.

The Comprehensive Development and Land Use Plan for the Caño Martín Peña

Special Planning District (Development Plan), created with the active and informed participation of the residents, made it clear that for its implementation to be possible the community had to have control of the land. Of the approximately 188 hectares (466 acres) that comprise the Planning District, 78 hectares (194 acres), were scattered throughout and were owned by five different governmental entities. Although there were some vacant lots and public buildings, most of this acreage was occupied by residents lacking any kind of land title. The planned eco-restoration of the channel and rehabilitation of the District's infrastructure would have made these residents vulnerable to involuntary displacement and gentrification. That is why the Caño's communities held a long and thorough deliberation process to assess what kind of land ownership strategy might be available that would ensure the permanence of their communities (Algoed, Hernández-Torrales, Rodríguez Del Valle, 2018).

Within the Caño Martín Peña Special Planning District there had previously been different strategies and experiences regarding land ownership. At the beginning of this informal settlement, the peasants who occupied government-owned and publicly owned land without legal title became owners of the improvements on the land, but the land continued to be public or under the government's ownership.[5] During the 1960s and early 1970s, some of the Caño communities, with the government's assistance, formed land cooperatives that allowed many residents to acquire the land they occupied and to develop basic infrastructure for their communities. On July 1, 1975, the Puerto Rico Legislature enacted a law that made it possible for low-income families or individuals without land title, like residents of the communities along the Caño, to be able to acquire the title to public land at a very low cost, mostly for just one dollar (US$1.00). This measure was used by politicians as a clientelist strategy, however, to gain electoral votes and not all community residents benefited from the law.

By the year 2002, there were homeowners in the Caño communities who had individual title to their land, but almost fifty percent of the Caño's residents were still living on land over which they had neither ownership nor control. Residents realized that, because of the strategic location of their neighborhoods, restoring the Caño would further encourage the sale of plots of land with titles to speculators at higher prices than their market value, but significantly below their market potential, and continue to fragment the communities. Those who sold their plots would not be able to find alternative housing within the city for the money they had received for their land.

As part of the participatory planning, action, and reflection process that led to the eventual adoption of the Development Plan, residents evaluated various options to address insecurity of tenure against a set of priorities that included: avoiding displacement and gentrification as an unintended consequence of restoring the Caño; getting access to credit; and ensuring their heirs could inherit the right to occupy and use the land, supported by a valid title. Residents considered those forms of land ownership they already were familiar with, such as individual land titles and land cooperatives, and also explored ways of owning and managing land that were new to Puerto Rico, including the community land trust.

After thorough consideration, they found the CLT to be an instrument that is flexible enough to fulfill their needs and more. Three basic characteristics distinguished the CLT from other forms of ownership, namely community-led development on community-owned land for the provision of affordable housing for low-income families. Within

> The Caño's residents designed a CLT that would enable them to achieve security of tenure.

that general framework, the CLT could be adapted and applied in any way a community might prefer. In the Caño's case, the residents concluded that a CLT would allow them to have collective control over the land and would ensure implementation of the Development Plan, including providing housing for families in need of relocation. The Caño's residents designed a CLT that would enable them to achieve security of tenure and to regularize their relationship with the land beneath their houses. Through the *Fideicomiso de la Tierra del Caño Martín Peña*, their right to use the land would be validated through a legal document (a deed) that recognized their right to use the surface of the land; that right would be inheritable under Puerto Rico's laws; the improvements (the house) would be registered at the Puerto Rico Registry of Real Estate Property, together with the surface rights deed; residents would be able to develop new housing; and they would have access to mortgage credit, among other important benefits they had not previously enjoyed.[6]

The Legal Framework of the Caño Martín Peña CLT

The CLT is a variable tool, allowing wide possibilities of adaptation according to the conditions of the legal system of each country. Puerto Rico was a Spanish colony until it was invaded by the United States in 1898. This caused a change of jurisdiction in legal terms. In the areas of private law (e.g., persons, property ownership and its modifications, different ways of acquiring ownership, obligations and contracts), Puerto Rico still applies fundamentals of the Spanish Civil Code, as do most Latin American countries. However, in areas such as corporate law, administrative law, and constitutional law, Puerto Rico uses the Anglo-Saxon common law as a primary reference.

Securing community control of the Caño's publicly owned land was critical for the implementation of the Development Plan and to provide housing for those residents who needed to be relocated to provide the physical space for the infrastructure projects. The costs of all the work planned for the dredging of the channel and rehabilitation of the Caño communities was initially estimated at $700 million, but Puerto Rico soon started to suffer from a severe economic and fiscal crisis that has now extended for more than fifteen years. Hence, in order to ensure the implementation of the Development Plan and to alleviate costs, it was essential not only that all public land within the Special Plan-ning District would be put under the control of the organized communities, but that the cost to the communities of acquiring the land would be negligible. Otherwise, the cost of completing the Caño infrastructure projects would be rendered unbearable.

These considerations led the organized communities of the Caño to decide not to create the Caño CLT as a nonprofit corporation under the Puerto Rico General Corpo-rations Law. Instead, the Caño communities decided to draft a bill that would create their CLT as a trusteeship, along with all the other instruments needed for implementation of the Development Plan. Among the other purposes of this innovative strategy, enactment of this special law by the government of Puerto Rico would enable the free transfer of public land to the Caño CLT.

Law 489-2004, as amended, gave life to the *Proyecto ENLACE del Caño Martín Peña* as an independent project. It also created the tools needed for its implementation. The legis-lation created a government corporation, the ENLACE Project Corporation (ENLACE). This new corporation was charged with responsibility for coordinating the dredging of the Martín Peña Channel. It would also be responsible for coordinating the rehabilitation and new construction of infrastructure (stormwater and sanitary sewers, potable water systems), the relocation of power lines, streets, and public spaces, and the relocation of families and housing. These interventions were deemed crucial not only for the ecologi-cal restoration of the channel, but also to reduce the risk of flooding with polluted water that recurrently affected the communities. The ENLACE Corporation was charged with creating the conditions for the economic and social development of the Caño commu-nities as well.[7]

The Fideicomiso de la Tierra del Caño Martín Peña (Caño Martín Peña CLT) was also created by means of Law 489-2004 as a private legal entity, separate from ENLACE or from any other governmental agency or instrumentality, and was invested with the legal authority to fulfill its responsibilities. All the public land within the Special District was transferred by this Law to ENLACE, which then transferred the land to the CLT by means of public deeds.

The Caño Martín Peña CLT is governed by regulations and by a board of trustees designed by the residents as a result of a two-year participatory planning process. The composition of this board differs somewhat from the three-part model used by most CLTs in the United States. Residents of the Caño communities decided that they would retain a majority of the seats on the governing board, while still providing for represen-tation by the government and by other parties who are not residents of the Caño. The CLT's eleven-member board of trustees is constituted as follows: four are individuals residing on CLT land, elected by their peers; two are community residents, delegated by G-8, a coalition of community-based organizations representing all of the Caño's neigh-borhoods; two are experts, selected by the board, according to the organization's needs;

two are representatives of governmental agencies;[8] and one is a representative of the municipality of San Juan.

A Proposed Legal Framework for Brazilian CLTs

The Caño Martín Peña CLT provided the comparative starting point for Catalytic Communities' own research into how a CLT might be established in Brazil. As CLT practitioners around the world have discovered, the model and instruments developed in one country must be modified to conform to laws and politics in another country. That is true in the Brazilian case as well.

The trusteeship (*fideicomiso*) used by the Caño Martín Peña CLT, for example, which was established through an act of the legislature in Puerto Rico, cannot be used for the purpose of establishing a CLT in Brazil, unless a specific law were to be adopted. Any attempt to enact such a law would run into political and bureaucratic difficulties. Even so, CatComm and organizers in favela communities may eventually pursue the presentation of a CLT bill as a political strategy to foster debate on the issue. They would propose a model that is able not only to guarantee security of tenure, but also to integrate the community and to increase its capacity for self-management and political negotiation.

But, for now, an arrangement was sought using instruments already existing in the Brazilian legal system which are capable of providing the basis for the present-day implementation of a Brazilian model of the community land trust, tailored to local specifications and needs. A legal framework was developed and proposed by CatComm that unites several instruments for the construction of a community land trust that could be specifically applied to addressing the problem of land insecurity in the favelas of Rio de Janeiro. This legal framework for a Brazilian CLT has three components, which may be assembled sequentially in different stages or pursued on parallel tracks. They are as follows:

- Acquisition of land and regularization of title by community residents;

- Constitution of the legal entity to receive the land and to be responsible for the continuing ownership and management of the land; and

- Separation of ownership of buildings from the ownership of land, transferring surface rights back to community members who manage the legal entity that owns the land.

Land acquisition and regularization. The legal reality in Rio's informal settlements, as well as in favelas throughout Brazil, is of people occupying land for which they have neither ownership nor control. Sometimes this land has not even been registered. Considering that the community land trust relies on gaining possession of land, where the ownership of lands and buildings will then be separated, the regularization and registration of title and the transfer of ownership are indispensable for the implementation of a CLT. There are many instruments for the regularization and conveyance of land in Brazil. The most significant in terms of dealing with land insecurity in informal settlements are adverse possession, concession of use, donation, purchase and sale, and land legitimization.

- *Adverse possession (usucapião)* is used for the acquisition of titles of property by populations residing on privately owned land. The basic argument is that the registered owners have failed to fulfill the social function of the property for a certain period of time, stipulated by law, during which the residents occupied the property and, as a result of continuous occupation over many years, they now have a legal claim to that land.

- *Concession of use* is an instrument that usually applies to publicly owned land, where it is not possible to apply adverse possession. This is an administrative contract that grants the use of a property for a certain period of time. Generally, in order to provide the instrument with more security, concessions have a 99-year term that can be extended for an equal period.

- *Donation* is an instrument through which public or private owners donate, free of charge, the land inhabited by low-income residents to said residents.

- *Purchase and sale* demands a financial contribution from the residents.

- *Land legitimization* is a new instrument provided by Law 13.465 (2017), which was intended to become the main land regularization instrument in Brazil. Applicable in public or private areas, it seeks to ensure private property for residents of informal occupations, be they low-income or otherwise.

Constitution of a legal entity. With the use of one of these instruments, once title is regularized and the ownership of land is poised to be conveyed to a community land trust, there must be a legal entity in place to constitute the CLT, receiving title and becoming responsible for the ownership and management of the land for years to come. This legal entity may take various forms (e.g. association, condominium, etc.) in accordance with the Brazilian legal system. A case-by-case analysis will be required to decide the best format in a specific situation. CatComm's analysis has recommended that each CLT be established as a nonprofit legal entity with a dual objective of holding and managing land on behalf of a particular favela and preserving its affordability for low-income residents.

Separating land ownership and building ownership. Once these other stages have been achieved, the ownership of any buildings already existing on the land when it was acquired by the CLT, and, typically, the ownership of future buildings constructed on the land, must be separated from ownership of the underlying land. (The legal entity that owns the land—i.e., the CLT—must, in turn, be collectively controlled by residents who live on the land.) When it comes to the separation of ownership, there are several instruments available in the Brazilian legal system. The most appropriate of them, as concluded by CatComm's analysis, will be the surface rights deed, similar to what is being used by the Caño CLT in Puerto Rico.

With the separation of ownership, the three components of the legal constitution of a Brazilian CLT would be put in place. The crafting of each component will then depend upon the objectives and needs of the communities that are building the model. What is presented here is only a basic legal framework, which offers several options suitable to serve the diverse needs that will present themselves in practice.

Coming to the end of this legal sequence, the CLT will be able to exert its full potential in the territory it has chosen to serve. Especially based on a collective management model designed by the community according to its own needs and specificities, the CLT will be able to recognize local realities and to strengthen community assets as it seeks territorial improvements.

This methodology releases any CLT implementation from the need to wait or to depend on the approval of enabling legislation, which could take years considering the unstable Brazilian political scene. That said, the fight for specific CLT enabling legislation should be pursued in parallel to the application of existing instruments described above, since legislative support could significantly facilitate, support, and boost efforts to establish favela CLTs.[9]

The CLT is seen by a growing number of favela leaders, NGOs, legal experts, practitioners, academics, and public servants in the urban planning and land titling fields in Rio, as a *ferramenta de costura*, a "seaming tool" that integrates and addresses diverse conclusions reached separately over the years by residents and supporters working on supportively addressing the problem of informality. CLTs provide a foundation for:

- securing the social function of land;

- realizing the need for land regularization;

- respecting the typology and self-management already inherent in favelas;

- promoting and preserving the affordability of housing;

- respecting people's sense of belonging and deeper concern for permanence (rather than seeing homes as a "speculative investment");

- recognizing the importance of community-controlled, participatory planning processes;

- guaranteeing a re-ordering of the community, so that services can be provided, consistent with a "do no harm" approach; and

◾ engaging technical expertise in support of community planning, rather than through top-down models.

III. GUIDELINES WHEN CONSIDERING A CLT AS A POSSIBLE STRATEGY FOR REGULARIZING LAND TENURE AND PROTECTING HOMES IN INFORMAL SETTLEMENTS

The collaborative research project that was conducted by CatComm and the Caño Martín Peña CLT involved peer-to-peer exchanges between community leaders and staff of the Caño Martín Peña CLT and interested favela communities and professionals during five days in Rio de Janeiro in August 2018. From that collaboration, we tentatively offer guidelines and recommendations for other communities that might be interested in implementing a similar strategy in their own territory.

It should be noted that every community is different and, therefore, every CLT will also be different. There is no universal recipe as to how to create one. Community residents design the bylaws, policies, priorities, and internal procedures, which will define the CLT and will be different for every new CLT in accordance with the community's particularities, circumstances, and needs. It is worth repeating, as well, that a CLT that is designed to address the challenges of regularizing land tenure in informal settlements will be organized and operated differently from a CLT freshly created to provide new housing in neighborhoods where ownership of the land is already formal(ized). Our recommendations are aimed, in fact, at neighborhoods like Brazil's favelas where people have

Fig. 3.5. Delegation from the Caño Martín Peña visiting the Barrinha favela, August 2018.
CATALYTIC COMMUNITIES

occupied land for years which they neither own nor control. In such settlements, activists who are interested in creating a CLT must consider two questions: What are the *conditions* that must be present to make a CLT feasible in an informal settlement; and what is the *process* that organizers must follow to make a CLT a reality?

Conditions: Where Might It Be Feasible to Establish a CLT in an Informal Settlement?

Community leaders and activists, public officials or others interested in developing CLTs should take into account that CLTs may not work in every community. For a CLT to be considered in the first place, as a possible strategy for addressing the need for regularization and upgrading in Rio de Janeiro's favelas — and, for that matter, in the informal settlements of many other countries — the following conditions need to be present:

* Consolidated communities are located on lands where residents perceive a threat — or experience the reality — of gentrification, forced eviction, or other human-induced involuntary displacement;

* A large percentage of families lack legal titles and want to address the problem of insecure land tenure;

* There is a possible path to acquiring title(s) to the land;

* Residents feel a strong sense of belonging and a desire to remain in their community; and

* There is a solid process of community organization in place, supported by organizations that are ready to accompany the community and that are able to provide technical assistance.

The experience of Puerto Rico and discussions to date in Brazil reveal that there are additional conditions that may be essential to the process of establishing a CLT in informal settlements. Amongst them are:

1. An organized community and mature leadership that fosters horizontal participation, new leadership and decision-making among all sectors, and that is willing to assume new responsibilities and to make a commitment that will last the life of the community.

2. Supportive organizations and technical allies that are prepared to: (a) accompany the community in strengthening an organizing process and, if necessary, to facilitate and to provoke difficult conversations that will ensure that the participatory planning, action, and continuous reflection process needed to choose and implement a CLT will be controlled by the community and have widespread participation; (b) engage

in dialogues with residents to help inform their decision-making process, where the technical allies are willing to both listen and to learn from the residents and to share their knowledge; and (c) help to strengthen and to complement the community and economic resources that are required to fulfill the community's development plan.

3. Community planning that comes first. CLTs that are designed to regularize land tenure must emerge and develop from existing resident desires and demands. Residents must come together to evaluate their options and make an active choice to adopt a CLT, and that CLT must provide a path to addressing their very real needs. Residents must also reach a broad understanding that some form of collective or community ownership of the land will best serve their needs and will allow them to accomplish their development objectives, both social and economic.

4. Communities that have a strong sense of belonging. The Caño's leaders made it clear that residents with this strong sense of belonging are those that are the most supportive of their own CLT, and that the pride in one's community and a strong sense of history can be strengthened and stimulated in the process or creating a CLT.

5. A legal entity that is controlled by the community, which can receive land rights as a means of collective or community ownership, along with the mechanisms to make the transfer a reality.

These five conditions are key to a successful CLT, but not all of them need to be present at the first moment of considering whether or not to form a CLT. In fact, several get put in place during the process of mobilization and reflection leading up to the decision to move forward in establishing this instrument. What should be emphasized and observed in every case of creating and applying a CLT in an informal settlement is community initiative and broad participation, both in the design of the CLT and in the definition of the goals to be achieved.

Process: How Might Residents Get Started in Establishing a CLT in an Informal Settlement?

As a result of the peer-to-peer exchanges between community leaders and staff of the Caño Martín Peña CLT and interested favela communities and professionals, a number of recommendations were made on essential steps to be taken when considering the formation of a new CLT in an informal settlement.

Start a process of community planning-action-reflection. Before anything else, residents have to decide whether a CLT is the right mechanism for land regularization in their community. A thorough process of planning with active and continuous resident participation is crucial to make informed decisions about the type of land tenure that will best serve their needs and, if it is decided that a CLT is the right mechanism, how the CLT will be established and governed and how the land will be managed as a collective asset to realize the community's vision. A *CLT is not an end in itself, but rather an instrument to achieve the goals of the community.*

In the Caño, residents engaged in a participatory planning–action–reflection process, where through concrete actions they could obtain short-term wins to keep the community engaged, and continuously reflect on their actions so as to learn from them and inform their planning process. Such a process can be started by residents, community leaders, community-based organizations, government agencies or NGOs. In every case, however, supportive technical allies must recognize their role as being one of helping to create the conditions that will enable residents to strengthen their organizations, to take control of the process, and to participate effectively.

Further recommendations for this participatory process include:

- Start small. Think from less to more. Sports or cultural events can help as a mobilizing method.

- Get residents involved who are influential in the community and who are trusted by a wide range of residents.

- Organize events where residents can think of their ideal community and define what they want their neighborhood to become.

- Develop and use popular education techniques such as street theater, comic books, videos, and others, and engage youth in their design and as communicators.

- Remember that it always seems impossible until it is done.

Create CLT structures, policies, and procedures. If it is decided that the CLT is the right mechanism to meet the needs of the community, residents need to decide how the CLT will function. The bylaws, policies, and activities of every CLT will be somewhat different. Residents must formulate what the shape and function of their CLT should be, which may change over time when conditions or contexts change. The organizational structures and operational priorities of other CLTs can be consulted as inspiration. (See, for example, the rules and regulations of the Caño CLT in "Reglamento General para el Funcionamiento del Fideicomiso de la Tierra del Caño Martín Peña," 2008.)

Technical assistance from professionals. NGOs, universities, or government will be necessary to support residents in achieving their goals. Professionals — social workers, urban planners, architects, engineers, lawyers — should support the process, not lead it. They are not the ones to provide answers to questions, as the knowledge lies within the community. Rather, they can help to expand possibilities. Social workers and community organizers that accompany the community can help facilitate discussions, find alternative ways to engage residents, promote critical thinking, and ensure that participation is productive and inclusive. Planners can help the community to keep a comprehensive perspective throughout the process. Engage experts after residents have defined what they need and what they want. If experts come too early or without proper orientation to promote a balanced dialogue, they may downplay the community, co-opt the process, or impose their own standards on communities.

Define the legal possibilities. After the community has defined what it wants, lawyers can get involved to guide the community through which legal instruments already exist that make the transformations legally possible. If certain legal instruments do not yet exist, they can be created to meet the needs of the community, or elements can be borrowed from other legal instruments. Also here, residents themselves must design these new legal instruments, with the help of lawyers (not the other way around). If elements are taken from existing legal instruments, it is essential to focus on the final goal and to make adjustments in the process in order to ensure the community's goal is reached. If members of a community have decided they want to hold their land collectively, for example, but their only legal option is to pass through individual titles first (as is currently the case in Brazil for publicly-owned lands), it will be necessary for residents to have reached a decisive conclusion to combine their titles under a CLT well prior to receiving those titles, and execute that decision immediately. Otherwise, speculation can curtail the process. Ideally, in this case, the CLT organization should be established in advance and be ready to receive those titles as soon as they are issued.

Strategize. The process to establish and to maintain a CLT requires continuous organizing and strategizing on how to choose partners and on how to communicate and to engage with third parties in order to achieve such objectives as securing the land, dealing with conflicts, and attracting resources, among others. Taking the time to stop and to reflect on the challenges and opportunities within and beyond the community is key to developing a successful path forward.

⁓

Community land trusts are always unique. The Caño CLT borrowed some elements from other CLTs, but residents and their allies also created many new elements completely from scratch in order to address the needs of their community and to find ways to make their CLT function properly within their own context. CLTs in Brazil will undoubtedly take on a whole new shape, and will differ from community to community, depending on the goals of residents and the circumstances of each community.

It is essential to remember, however, that there should never be discussions about the community — including discussions about forming a CLT — without the community being present. As organizers in informal settlements, from Johannesburg to Rio, often say: "Nothing for us, without us."

At the time this essay is being written, a working group comprised of 154 community leaders and technical allies has formed in Rio de Janeiro and is supporting the development of pilot CLTs in two communities that meet the conditions described above: the Trapicheiros and Esperança communities. This working group is also developing enabling legislative proposals and outreach materials to share the CLT model with other communities. Trapicheiros and Esperança have each embarked on the process of establishing their own CLT and are currently holding regular community social events and workshops, engaging residents in a participatory planning process towards forming a CLT.

The working group formed after the August 2018 visit by a delegation of five Caño Martín Peña CLT organizers, who came to Rio to share their story. This city-wide, multi-partner working group includes leaders from over twenty communities, land rights agents from the state, planners and lawyers from Rio's universities, public defenders, NGOs and others. Some of them traveled to Puerto Rico in May 2019 to participate in a peer-to-peer exchange hosted by the Caño Martín Peña communities. Community leaders and their support organizations from Argentina, Bangladesh, Barbuda, Belize, Bolivia, Brazil, Chile, Ecuador, Jamaica, Lebanon, Mexico, Peru, South Africa, and the United States came to San Juan learn more about the Caño CLT.

Seeds are being sown for new CLTs across the world. To be continued!

Notes

1. The study was financed by the Latin America program of the Lincoln Institute of Land Policy.

2. We are focusing here on the informal occupancy of land as an *urban* phenomenon. Throughout the world, however, there are also millions of acres of *rural* land that are occupied and used for housing, farming, grazing, and woodcutting by people who have no formal title to these lands.

3. In recent years, twelve favelas have opened museums documenting their histories. The social museology movement is growing.

4. The land law of 1850 established purchase-and-sale as a form of land acquisition in Brazil, breaking with the previous model that had recognized effective occupation of a territory as a criterion of acquisition. In addition, it provided for a system of land registration aimed at the formal regularization of the national territory, which was not applied in practice, however.

5. Original inhabitants built their homes themselves. Over time, as people moved on, houses were sold using informal documents or private contracts that clearly established that the buyer was only acquiring the house, not the land. Almost all of those documents stated that the land was public land. None of the documents were registered, however, which precluded buyers from accessing mortgage credit.

6. From a procedural perspective, the Caño Martín Peña opted for a surface rights deed, instead of a ground lease, for regularizing use of the land and for securing and registering a family's ownership of the house. A ground lease agreement may be used for other owners, however, like businesses or organizations established on the CLT's land.

7. This government corporation was set up with a sunset provision. It is scheduled to go out of business after twenty-five years.

8. One of these should be a board member of the ENLACE Project Corporation.

9. In effect, there are two possible legal ways to enable the formation of a CLT in informal settlements: (1) the approval of a specific law, detailing a CLT's application and creating legal instruments to put the CLT into effect; or (2) the use of instruments already existing in the legal system, combining several of them for the CLT's formation and operation.

References

Algoed, L., A. Cotté Morales, T. Fidalgo Ribeiro, M.E. Hernández Torrales, L. Rodriguez Del Valle and T. Williamson (forthcoming). Community Land Trusts and Informal Settlements: Assessing the feasibility of CLT instruments developed by the Caño Martin Peña communities in Puerto Rico for Favelas in Rio de Janeiro, Brazil. Working Paper. Cambridge: Lincoln Institute of Land Policy.

Algoed, L., M.E. Hernández Torrales and L. Rodríguez Del Valle (2018). El Fideicomiso de la Tierra del Caño Martín Peña: Instrumento Notable de Regularización de Suelo en Asentamientos Informales, Working Paper. Cambridge: Lincoln Institute of Land Policy.

Corporación del Proyecto ENLACE del Caño Martín Peña (2008). Reglamento general para el funcionamiento del Fideicomiso de la Tierra, Núm. 7587. San Juan: Departamento de Estado.

Children Win (2016). *Rio 2016 Olympics: The Exclusion Games.* https://www.childrenwin. org/wp-content/uploads/2015/12/DossieComiteRio2015_ENG_web_ok_low.pdf

Ministério das Cidades. Regularização Fundiária Urbana—Lei 13.465/17. Accessed March 12, 2019. http://www.cohab.mg.gov.br/wp-content/uploads/2017/11/Reurb-out..pdf

Osborne, C (2013). "A History of Favela Upgrades Part III: Morar Carioca in Visio and Practice (2008–2013)." *RioOnWatch*, April 2. *https://www.rioonwatch.org/?p=8136*

Robertson, D. and T. Williamson (2017). "The Favela as a Community Land Trust: A Solution to Eviction and Gentrification?" *Progressive City*, May 2. *https://catcomm.org/law-clt/*

Soares, G. R. (2009). "Repensar a regularização fundiária como política de integração socioespacial." *Estudos Avançados* Vol. 23 No. 66. http://www.scielo.br/scielo.php?script=sci_arttext&pid=S0103-40142009000200017

Timerman, J. (2013). "Is a Favela Still a Favela Once It Starts Gentrifying?" *CityLab*, December 2. *https://www.citylab.com/equity/2013/12/favela-still-favela-once-it-starts-gentrifying/7726/*

Williamson, T. D. (2015). "A new threat to favelas: gentrification." *Architectural Review*, May 30. *https://www.architectural-review.com/opinion/a-new-threat-to-favelas-gentrification/8682967.article*

Williamson, T. D. (2018). "Community Land Trusts in Rio's Favelas: Could Community Land Trusts in Informal Settlements Help Solve the World's Affordable Housing Crisis?" *Land Lines*, July 31. *https://www.lincolninst.edu/sites/default/files/pubfiles/land-lines-july-2018-full_2.pdf*

Williamson, T. D. (2020). "Favela vs. Asphalt: Suggesting a New Lens on Rio de Janeiro's Favelas and Formal City," *Comparative Approaches To Informal Housing Around The Globe*, edited by Udo Grashoff. London: UCL Press.

Williamson, T. D. (forthcoming). "Proporcionar seguridad de tenencia para los actuales habitantes del barrio," *Barrio 31,* los inicios de una operación transformadora, edited by Agustina Gonzalez Cid. Washington, DC: Inter-American Development Bank.

Williamson, T. D. (2017). "Rio's Favelas: The Power of Informal Urbanism." *Perspecta 50: Urban Divides,* M. McAllister and M. Sabbagh (editors). Cambridge: MIT Press, September.

Williamson, T. D. (2019). "The Favela Community Land Trust: A Sustainable Housing Model for the Global South," *Critical Care: Architecture and Urbanism for a Broken Planet,* Angelika Fitz and Elke Krasny (editors). Cambridge: MIT Press.

4.

A Watershed Land Trust in Honduras

Profile of Fundación Eco Verde Sostenible

Kirby White and Nola White

The Honduran nonprofit organization known as FECOVESO (*Fundación Eco Verde Sostenible*) serves rural communities in northwest Honduras. Financial support for these services is provided by a charitable nonprofit in the United States, the Honduras Community Support Corporation. FECOVESO is a specialized community land trust that acquires and holds parcels of land surrounding the water sources for gravity-feed systems serving small mountain communities. FECOVESO also functions as a funding vehicle for a variety of community development projects in these and other small communities in the region.

BACKGROUND

The origins of FECOVESO can be traced to the early 1990s, when a Peace Corps volunteer named Nola White was sent to Honduras to assist with the development of gravity-feed water systems in mountain communities in the northwest. Until then, water for local households had been carried from nearby streams, usually in large jars borne on the heads of women. The Peace Corps and the Honduran Government provided materials and technical assistance to build these systems. The physical labor was provided by residents of the communities themselves. Nola's role involved initiating, organizing, and supporting these projects in one community after another. It was a role for which she was exceptionally well-qualified through her social skills and her previous experience as a community organizer in the USA.

Three years with the Peace Corps left her with many friends in Honduras. She returned a number of times in the next few years to visit the communities where she had worked, as well as neighboring ones. These were not only social visits, however; she also became increasingly involved in supporting a variety of community development projects in the places she visited, acquiring watersheds, improving water systems, and constructing schools. She was known locally as "the *gringa* who came back."

It quickly became apparent that these projects needed funding that was going to be impossible to find in Honduras, so she recruited friends and family to establish a non-profit organization in the United States to serve as a vehicle for raising funds in the USA that could be directed to projects in Honduras. The Honduras Community Support Corporation (HCSC) was founded in 2002. She then worked with community leaders and others in Honduras to establish a second nonprofit, *Fundacion Eco Verde Sostenible* (FECOVESO). The dual mission of this Honduran organization was to manage and to allocate funds received from HCSC and to function as a regional land trust, perma-nently protecting the water sources and watersheds on which community water systems depended.

THE REGION AND ITS COMMUNITIES

The mountainous region served by FECOVESO measures roughly 60 kilometers from north to south and 60 kilometers from east to west. It is bounded on the north by the Caribbean Sea, on the west by the Guatemala border, on the east by the highway between the port city of Puerto Cortez and the inland industrial city of San Pedro Sula, and on the south (roughly) by the height of land between the north and south slopes of the moun-tain range. Except for the fringes along the coastal highway and the Puerto Cortez-San Pedro Highway, the entire region is off the national electric grid. It is also roadless, except for a few *caminos* that are more or less passable for four-wheel-drive vehicles, but are used mostly by people on foot or on horse-or-mule-back.

By modern standards of countries in the Global North, the people living in the small communities scattered throughout this rural region in Honduras would be seen as deeply "deprived" and extremely "poor." They live very much as people have lived in these moun-tains for countless generations — without motor vehicles, without electricity and, for the most part, without money. Yet, in some important ways, they are much better off than the majority of Honduran city-dwellers, who are beset by varying degrees of physical insecu-rity, violence, displacement, and potential starvation.

The mountain people live in circumstances that may not appear to offer many ben-efits — the homes in each community are widely scattered, with no recognizable street grid, no stores (the nearest store may be a day's walk away), and no regular medical ser-vices (the nearest clinic may also be a day's walk away). What these people do have is the security, connections, and comfort of living in genuine communities. They know who all of their neighbors are, who all of their neighbors' relatives are, and how the various extended families within the community are interrelated. (One of the communities with which FECOVESO has worked is called *Los Mejias* — *Mejia* being the last name of most of the people in the community.) As a resident of such a community you may or may

Fig. 4.1. Honduras mountains. SUSAN ALANCRAIG

not like all your neighbors and relatives, but you are unlikely to fear them. And if you need help, it is likely they will do what they can for you. There is real security in such a community.

There is also security in the kind of homeownership such people have, even though very few of them hold what others would recognize as secure legal title to their homes. In some cases, their ownership rights are based on no more than their neighbors' acknowledgement that "the family has always lived there." In other cases, they may have a written record of the property having been sold to them — the equivalent of a quitclaim deed in what is likely to be a long chain of unrecorded quitclaim deeds. If some wealthier person were to have a financial motive for legally dislodging them, it would be quite easy to do, but this rarely happens.

The dwellings that the mountain people have on such properties are, by most standards, primitive. Some of them are traditional "bajareque" (mud and stick) structures with thatched roofs. Others are built with planks slabbed from local timber with a chainsaw, and roofed with (typically recycled) metal sheeting. Most homes have hard-packed dirt floors. Cooking is done on wood-fired stoves, which also provide some comfort during chilly days in the rainy season — though the climate is relatively mild year-round.

The diet of the mountain people, like their shelter, is simple and sufficient. Corn and beans are the core of their diet. A household's corn is typically grown in small patches of approximately an acre in size (sometimes some distance from the household's dwelling); beans are more often grown in dooryard gardens. All crops are cultivated with a hoe. When corn is harvested, the ears are usually stored, still in their dried husks, on overhead racks in the stove-dried kitchen area — to be shucked and shelled as they are needed. The shelling is likely to be done by a woman sitting in the kitchen door with a pan in her lap, and typically with the dooryard chickens gathered around to chase after any kernels that escape the pan. The shelled corn is then ground in a hand-cranked grinder — the cranking of which is one of the many tasks that typically fall to the children of the house. Meat is rarely a part of the diet. But there are many kinds of fruit — including citrus, bananas, avocados, mangos, papayas, coconuts, and more — that can be grown in the dooryard or gathered from where they grow wild, and there are always kids who know where things grow and are ready to climb the trees and pick what's ripe.

This way of life remains mostly as it has been for many generations. The one thing that is new, for the more fortunate of these remote communities, is that water is now piped directly to each family's home. This benefit is provided by gravity-feed water systems that typically collect water from small streams, which have been dammed to create retention pools as high in the watershed as possible.

FECOVESO AS A LAND TRUST

A majority of the funding that FECOVESO receives from HCSC has been used to purchase watershed lands that surround the sources of water for these mountain communities. Control of such lands is crucial, because larger parcels tend to be owned by non-residents whose interest in the land is likely to include commercial cattle grazing and logging, uses that are not in the best interest of the people who live nearby. Honduran law does give local communities a collective right to draw water from springs or streams on private land. It is virtually impossible, however, for these communities to protect the quality of

> There are practical reasons for vesting ownership of watershed lands in a regional stewardship institution.

this water against the polluting effects of grazing and logging if they do not have control over the surrounding watershed, including not only the immediate pool from which the water is piped, but the more distant areas from which the water drains. To exert such control, the land in question must be held — in legally enforceable terms — either directly by the communities served or by a reliable stewardship institution, holding the property and protecting the water on a community's behalf.

Direct, collective ownership by the communities themselves is not practical in most cases. The communities are very small and are typically not incorporated, so they cannot hold recorded title to real property. Even if a community has been incorporated — as a few have been with FECOVESO's assistance — there are practical reasons for vesting ownership of watershed lands in a more extensive regional stewardship institution, rather than having these lands owned and managed by a very small community and governed by a board of supervisors (*patronado*) that is subject to all the complications of local politics.

Fig. 4.2. Water source for a mountain village, Honduras. SUSAN ALANCRAIG

FECOVESO's founders did consider the possibility of direct community ownership, but quickly decided in favor of ownership by a regional organization. The founders also considered the possibility of allowing certain other land uses on FECOVESO's watershed lands if such uses did not interfere with watershed protection. Here again, however, they chose not to involve the organization in the complicated process of deciding what did or what did not interfere with watershed protection in a particular locale. As a land trust, therefore, FECOVESO has a single, very specific purpose — to protect the watersheds on which households within the communities depend for their domestic water supply.

As of this writing, FECOVESO has acquired and presently holds 17 parcels of land, totaling about 376 acres, in watersheds supplying 15 water systems. (Some systems serve multiple communities.) The organization has also purchased fencing materials to protect otherwise unenclosed parcels, and has supported reforestation in some of the watersheds. Fencing and reforestation work is done by members of the communities being served by the water supply, although a substantial amount of reforestation work was done in one watershed by personnel from a nearby Honduran naval base.

FECOVESO AS A COMMUNITY DEVELOPMENT ORGANIZATION

Community development projects carried out by FECOVESO include the construction of new water systems and the expansion and repair of existing systems. (The U.S. Peace Corps is no longer doing such work in Honduras.) Other significant community development projects have included the construction, expansion, and repair of schools. These buildings are important to the communities not only in providing for elementary education, but also as community meeting places. FECOVESO has provided materials for constructing or expanding twelve schools, and for repairing nineteen others. It has provided desks, or the materials to make desks, for six schools. FECOVESO has also helped some communities to build or to improve basic medical facilities, to build footbridges over mountain streams and, in a few cases, to improve mountain roads so that four-wheel-drive vehicles can deliver materials to remote communities.

The nature of FECOVESO's role in such projects is defined by three important principles. First, the needs to be addressed by a project must be identified by community members themselves. Secondly, there must be evidence of community-wide support for the project. Lastly, the work required by the project must be carried out by community residents. (Exceptions are work that requires operating special equipment such as a bulldozer or work that requires special expertise, such as the masonry entailed in constructing a water tank.) FECOVESO's role is limited to covering the cost of necessary materials and to providing expertise that the community itself does not possess and cannot possibly pay for.

> The needs to be addressed by a project must be identified by community members themselves.

FECOVESO GOVERNANCE AND OPERATIONS

The Board of Directors for FECOVESO includes representatives of the communities where FECOVESO owns watershed land, plus other individuals with legal, financial, or technical expertise. (HCSC is not formally represented on the FECOVESO board, although Nola White serves on the boards of both organizations.) The governing board of FECOVESO meets monthly in an office facility located on a parcel of land that is owned by FECOVESO.

The organization's staff currently consists of two part-time employees, native Hondurans who are paid modest salaries. Nestor Lainez does the record-keeping for the organization and has extensive experience with water systems, building construction, and other practical matters. Marivel Reyes Ayalla is an attorney who deals with legal and financial matters for FECOVESO, functioning as the de facto executive director. She lives in a house immediately adjacent to the office.

Communities seeking assistance for either watershed protection or a community development project must submit a written proposal (*solicitud*) to FECOVESO's board, specifying the need to be addressed by the project and detailing the cost of meeting that need. The *solicitudes* are reviewed by a board committee that includes Nestor Lainez, who visits proposed sites and evaluates construction plans and budgets. Based on Nestor's analysis, the committee may recommend modifications of the proposed project to increase its effectiveness and/or to reduce its cost. Once satisfied that a proposed project meets FECOVESO's criteria, the committee presents the project to the full board of directors for consideration at its next monthly meeting. In reviewing a proposed project, the board takes into account not only the committee's recommendation but also the availability of funds at that point in the current fiscal year. In FECOVESO's early years, final approval for both watershed acquisitions and community development projects was given by the

HCSC board; however, the current practice provides annual "block grants" from HCSC to FECOVESO. All decisions determining how to allocate funds *within* Honduras are made by FECOVESO's board.

In supporting more expensive projects — such as those involving the purchase of larger parcels of land — FECOVESO has sometimes been able to partner with other institutions to put together the necessary funding. Most notably, it has been possible to leverage support for several projects from the *Municipalidad de Omoa*, which is the equivalent of a county government in the USA in its geographical extent and political function. Included within the jurisdiction of the *Municipalidad de Omoa* are most of the communities served by FECOVESO.

THE FUTURE OF FECOVESO

FECOVESO has come of age as an accomplished and sustainable organization. It has a strong track record and the respect of other institutions in Honduras. It is staffed, administered, and governed by Hondurans, who run the organization without the on-site presence of Nola White, who is now 82 years old and has begun cutting back on the three-to-four months of every year that she used to spend in Honduras.

Financially, however, FECOVESO still relies on HCSC, its organizational partner in the United States, for most of the funding that is needed to continue the current level of activity in Honduras. HCSC is staffed entirely with volunteers and has almost no administrative overhead, so nearly every dollar that is raised goes directly to support the projects and operations of FECOVESO (*http://www.hcsc-honduras.org*).

Fig. 4.3. FECOVESO board of directors, Honduras, 2019.

5.

Seeding the CLT in Africa

Lessons from the Early Efforts to Establish Community Land Trusts in Kenya

Claire Simonneau and Ellen Bassett,
with Emmanuel Midheme

Informal settlements remain one of the biggest challenges in urban Africa. These are under-serviced settlements that have developed through the unauthorized occupation of land (Huchzermeyer and Karam, 2006: 3).[1] Kenyan cities are no exception in this regard, since more than 50% of the urban population lives in such settlements (Syagga, 2011). Nairobi's informal settlements are renowned worldwide for their scale, density, and extremely poor living conditions relative to housing quality and access to water, electricity, sewerage, and solid waste disposal.[2]

Like most former colonies, Kenya inherited its land and planning laws from Europe — Great Britain in this case. It is a centralized system, initially serving the colonial project to conquer territories at the expense of indigenous people, which has enabled a deep-rooted patron-client relationship among the land administration and widespread corruption in the distribution of land to elites (Bassett, 2017). Such a legal framework has revealed itself to be incapable of dealing with the rapid urban growth that has been happening in Kenya since the 1960s. Public and private mechanisms for land and housing delivery have offered very limited supply and/or were inaccessible to the majority of urban dwellers.

As a result, informal settlements have become the only viable means for accessing land for housing for the urban majority (Durand-Lasserve, 1988; Gulyani and Bassett, 2007; Midheme, 2015). Diverse policies have been implemented to deal with this form of urbanization since the 1950s, with the substantial — although uneven — support of international development agencies.[3]

The Tanzania-Bondeni Community Land Trust emerged in 1994 as a reaction to these policy responses — and their failures. This experiment was deemed successful during its first decade.[4] The CLT still exists, but is far less renowned today. No other CLTs have been established in Kenya, nor in any other country on the African continent. One of the questions we will attempt to answer in this chapter, therefore, is what can be learned from the Tanzania-Bondeni experiment that might shed light on why CLT development has stalled in Kenya and in Africa in general.

We will examine the Tanzania-Bondeni Community Land Trust from several perspectives.[5] This chapter starts with a historical overview of governmental policy regarding the country's informal settlements. We will then describe the Tanzania-Bondeni CLT today, exploring its achievements and current challenges. In the final section, we will discuss the notion of community and its sustainability over time.

I. POLICY RESPONSES TO INFORMAL SETTLEMENTS IN KENYA

A brief historical overview of policy responses since the country's independence from Great Britain in 1963 provides a useful context for comprehending the emergence of the Tanzania-Bondeni Community Land Trust in Voi. These governmental responses fall into four periods, which reflect both national and international thinking regarding informal settlements, slum upgrading, and land and housing policies (Gulyani and Bassett, 2007; Jenkins, Smith, and Wang, 2007; Kamunyori, 2016; Midheme, 2018).

During the decades of the 1950s and 1960s, informal settlements were mostly ignored by national and municipal officials who put their money and remedial efforts into building public housing. This line of action was supported by the belief that informal settlements would gradually disappear with economic growth and public housing policies. However, the delivery of public housing was never able to keep pace with continuing growth of the urban population.

Through the 1970s and early 1980s, it became evident that informal settlements were not an ephemeral phenomenon. The central government engaged in slum clearance (demolition), with the paradoxical effect that informal settlements got rebuilt in other parts of the city, just relocating the problem, not actually solving it. Following the World Bank strategy of that time, relocation programs were then implemented through site and services schemes[6] or through low-cost building. Nevertheless, these programs failed to reach their objectives. Land-market pressure, coupled with political patronage and corruption in plot allocation, resulted in "filtering up"; that is, initial beneficiaries of such programs were replaced by better-off households and original slum dwellers moved into newly created informal settlements — again.

Thus ensued the third policy response, based on the idea that informal settlements should be upgraded rather than eliminated. This intervention gradually gained momentum both in international thinking and within the Kenyan government. Upgrading programs took different forms and addressed diverse issues, including provision of basic services, land tenure regularization, and infrastructure improvement. These upgrading programs were better adapted to local realities, but a number of criticisms were leveled at them, highlighting three main inadequacies. First, Kenyan informal settlements are

> Restrictions on resale in upgrad-
> ing programs were revealed to
> be both costly to implement
> and easy to circumvent.

characterized by a high proportion of tenants, a population that has rarely been taken
into consideration in upgrading programs.
Here is highlighted a particular feature of the
Kenyan land system: upon independence in
1963, Kenya embraced both capitalism and
private property and enacted policies to change customary tenures to leasehold or freehold, particularly in peri-urban areas. By contrast, in many other African countries land
access continued to be determined by customary systems of land tenure.[7] In Kenya, however, land has a market value. This is especially true in Nairobi where the land and buildings in informal settlements are characterized by a very high commercial value and there
exists a vibrant rental market (Kamunyori, 2016).

A second criticism of upgrading programs was the turnover in beneficiaries, who resold
lands and homes to which they had been granted title, either due to market pressures (voluntary or distress sales) or to reap a speculative windfall. This remained a conundrum.
Restrictions on resale that were imposed in upgrading programs were revealed to be both
costly to implement and easy to circumvent. Consequently, informal sales continued to
take place, creating a growing gap between official registration and actual landowners as
recognized on the ground. Third, there was poor involvement of targeted communities in
the design and implementation of upgrading programs, ignoring a potential resource that
might have enhanced the programs' efficiency.

The idea of a community land trust (CLT) was introduced in Kenya in the early
1990s, representing a fourth policy response to the problem of informal settlements. The
CLT was touted as a credible answer to the recurrent problems encountered in upgrading programs. The CLT model, as developed and applied in the USA, had two advantages over the way that upgrading had previously been done. First, the CLT had been
designed as an anti-speculation tool for reducing gentrification. Ownership of land and
ownership of structural improvements are separated. Land is held in trust in perpetuity
and not subject to speculation. Land-value appreciation is "locked" in the community,
while long-term land use rights are provided to individuals or households on a leasehold
basis. Second, the CLT model was considered a powerful vehicle for community empowerment, through community control of the land and community-based management of
the neighborhood. In this regard, it offered an interesting way to better involve dwellers
in upgrading programs, thus ensuring short-term upgrading achievement and long-term
community development.

These advantages attracted the attention of Kenya's Ministry for Local Government.
They also attracted interest and support from the German governmental organization for
technical cooperation (GTZ),[8] municipal officials of Voi town, and residents of an informal settlement in Voi named "Tanzania-Bondeni." This led eventually to the creation of
Africa's first and only CLT in the 1990s.

II. EARLY HISTORY OF THE TANZANIA-BONDENI CLT

Tanzania-Bondeni is an informal settlement located in Voi, a secondary town in Taita-Taveta County. The town had a population 13,000 inhabitants in 1989. Tanzania-Bondeni is located approximately 1.5 km from the city center and covers approximately 22 hectares (see Figure 14.1 below).

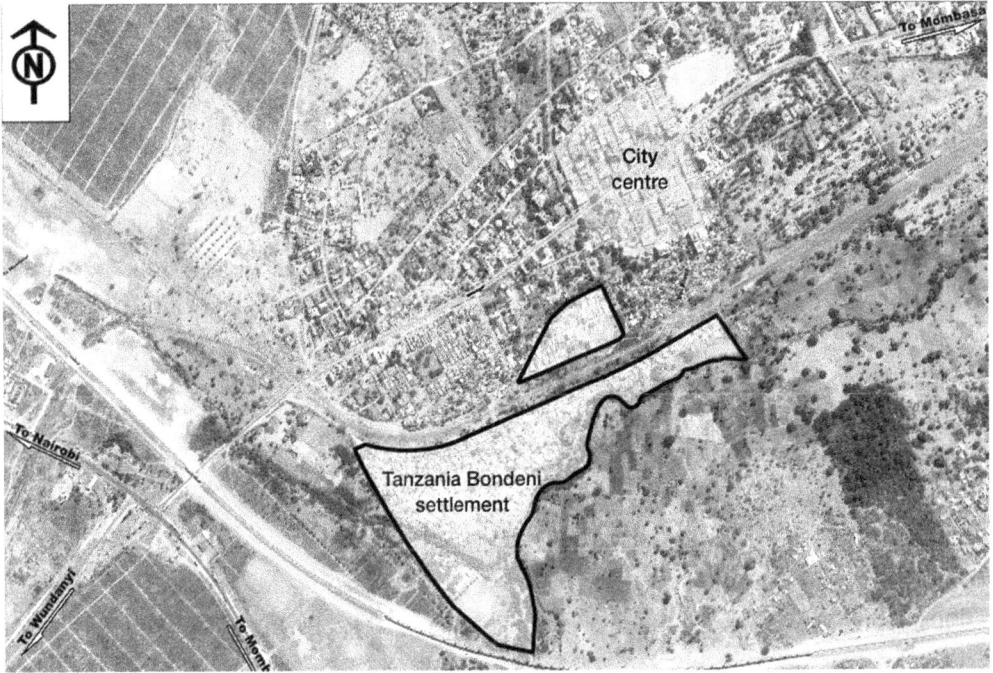

Fig. 5.1. Location of the informal settlement of Tanzania-Bondeni. Map scale: 1:10,000.
© SEVERIANO ODHIAMBO, MODIFIED BY CLAIRE SIMONNEAU

Nearly 3000 inhabitants were living in this informal settlement in 1990. Income levels were very low, with 70% of the inhabitants unemployed or earning less than $8 US a month. The community was quite heterogeneous in terms of ethnic background. The settlement had resulted from unauthorized occupation of public land — more precisely, land owned by Kenya Railways and Voi Sisal Estates, a large plantation growing sisal for industrial production (Bassett, 2001; Midheme and Moulaert, 2013). The condition of the settlement's housing was precarious. More than 60% of the houses were built with temporary materials like mud walls and thatch roofs. The settlement's other houses were made of semi-temporary materials — namely *but mabati* (corrugated iron) roofs and concrete floors.

Against this background, the Tanzania-Bondeni settlement was selected as a beneficiary of the Small Towns Development Project (STDP), an urban development program funded by the German government through GTZ. In its work in Voi, STDP had a tripartite steering committee composed of representatives from the Ministry for Local Government, the local authority of Voi town, and GTZ.

STDP clearly intended to innovate in the field of slum upgrading. After taking stock of the limits of previous approaches to squatter settlement, the project's managers gave careful attention to questions of land security and protections against eviction, including eviction by market forces. The project also benefited from reflections on innovative strategies for upgrading informal settlements that were conducted in the early 1990s by local, national, and international stakeholders. Several initiatives are worth mentioning.

In 1991, a national forum on alternative land tenure models in Kenya took place in Nairobi. It was held at the initiative of the Mazingira Institute, in conjunction with the Ford Foundation. The experience of CLTs in the United States was then presented. At the same time, a study was commissioned by the Ford Foundation to examine the potential for transferring the American CLT model to Kenya. Two American consultants, Chuck Matthei and Russell Hahn, were hired by Ford to conduct this study. They concluded, in light of the high housing demand and the prevalence of absentee ownership in low-income communities, that CLTs seemed relevant to Africa on the social and cultural level and could help in providing affordable housing in informal settlements (Matthei and Hahn, 1991). Over the next two years, an NGO called Kitua Cha Sheria (Legal Advice Center) engaged in the process of creating a CLT in a squatter settlement in Nairobi, based on the strategy of purchasing land on the market. The project was eventually abandoned, due to the excessive cost of acquiring land (Jaffer, 2000). In 1992, however, inspired by these previous events, STDP's program managers and the Project's national steering committee began considering the possibility of establishing a CLT in two other settlements that had been selected for upgrading: Mtaani-Kisumu Ndogo in Kilifi town and Tanzania-Bondeni in Voi town.

The upgrading sponsored by the Small Towns Development Project was meant to be participatory. It operated within a series of guidelines aimed at ensuring durable results and local ownership of the project. These guidelines called for gradual and systematic improvement of the neighborhood and full involvement of local communities in the planning and execution of the project. External actions and actors were meant to support local efforts, not replace them (Jaffer, 2000).

The land tenure option, in particular, was to be chosen by the community itself. A series of activities with the residents prepared for this vote, including preliminary community mobilization and the election of residents committees. In November 1992, a last discussion was held among planners of the Ministry and the STDP, the Voi municipal council, and members of the residents committees around three options for holding land in the informal settlements in Kilifi town and in Voi town: individual leasehold titles; individual titles coupled with housing cooperatives; or a group leasehold coupled with a community land trust. The resident committees in both towns held six community meetings dedicated to choosing among the three options. Attention was paid to helping residents fully understand all three options. STDP observers attended the meetings in order to ensure that only *bona fide* structure owners were allowed to vote and that both advantages and drawbacks of each option were thoroughly explained.[9]

The residents of Kilifi voted for individual titles. In Voi, however, over 90% of the structure owners finally opted for the CLT option. Jaffer (1996) documented the "push from below" in favor of the CLT option, which he observed in Voi. From the outset of the project, the Voi community demonstrated a great capacity for mobilization. The Voi resident committee, led by older long-term residents (*wazee* — elders), was fully informed of slum upgrading issues, including land issues. Local interest in the CLT also reflected a serious threat felt by the residents: land grabbing by outsiders — a phenomenon that had begun to occur in the neighborhood at the beginning of the upgrading project.[10] Residents were also attracted to the CLT option by: (1) the social security offered by community tenure and its protection against eviction by the market; (2) the possibility of keeping individual land rights within a community land tenure framework; and (3) the promise of having facilitated access to collective loans.

The decision was definitely related to the socio-economic situation of the Tanzania-Bondeni community. From interviews later conducted by Bassett (2001) and Midheme and Moulaert (2013), it can be seen that residents feared they would be unable to retain their land individually due to economic poverty and their lack of political power and patronage networks.[11] In other words, they felt they were too poor to pay for the costs associated with individual leaseholds (notably property taxes), and would be powerless to prevent "cashing out" behaviors within the community or by their own family. The Tanzania-Bondeni community also included numerous female-headed households. These women were attracted to the community control offered by CLT, since they considered it to be a way of protecting them from pressures within the family to sell the land (Bassett and Jacobs, 1997: 225).

GTZ and other institutional stakeholders such as the central and communal governments had their own reasons for promoting the CLT model: the avoidance of the "windfall effect" of upgrading projects; the prospect of community organization for other development partnerships; the prospect of extending financial sources, including property taxes; the upgrading of the slum; and the prevention of further squatting (Bassett and Jacobs, 1997). The decision of the Voi community was somewhat surprising for the central government and for STDP's project managers, however, given the overall preference for individual property in Kenya (Bassett, 2001: 164).

A. Complex Process of CLT Formalization

Once the CLT model had been chosen, its translation into Kenyan terms faced serious challenges. Four main legal issues emerged. To begin with, at that time Kenyan land law favored individual landholding. Communal landholding such as Group Ranches were reserved for specific regions in the country. Moreover, the legal form of the land trust was problematic, since incorporation in Kenya provided only for profit-making entities.

Lastly, the "rule against perpetuities" that exists in Kenyan law prevented anyone from holding the land outside of the market permanently, whereas this is one key objective of the CLT.

Lawyers had to find an innovative arrangement to overcome these obstacles. Two legal bodies were created in 1994: (1) a Settlement Society, registered under the Societies Act, representing the residents; and (2) a trust, registered under the Trustees (Perpetual Succession) Act, holding the land head-lease and administrating the land in conjunction with the Society, including decisions on land uses, alienation, and purchase of land. Through this latter body, the community applied for a head-lease; the CLT in turn was supposed to issue subleases to households (Bassett and Jacobs, 1997; Midheme and Moulaert, 2013).

The governance of the Tanzania-Bondeni Community Land Trust was structured around two main bodies: a Board of Trustees (9 members) that was to hold the head-lease and to grant subleases; and a Residents Committee (30 members) that was to run the daily affairs of the Settlement Society. An annual general meeting was the supreme body that approved audited accounts. Members were to pay annual fees to finance the recurrent spending of the Trust. In addition, four housing cooperatives were created at that time.

The Tanzania-Bondeni CLT in Voi also adopted conventional rules that were common in American CLTs such as preemptive rights of purchase by the CLT when a member leaves, and a restriction on absentee landlordism. Efforts were also made to accommodate the low-income situation of the residents: payments for collective services could be staggered; a local development fund was put in place to conduct local development projects; and, most importantly, the local government was persuaded to recognize existing dwellings within the settlement, even if they did not conform to existing building standards.[12]

B. Short-term Positive Impacts on the Whole Settlement

The creation of the CLT, along with additional interventions funded by STDP, had significant positive impacts in the short run. To begin with, the settlement benefited from physical planning that provided space for residential and commercial development, and also for community facilities.[13] This plan was developed with extensive input from the community and was rapidly implemented on the ground: houses were relocated, roads built, and infrastructure installed. Bassett and Jacobs (1997) also noticed that residents soon started to build with more durable materials or to plant long-term crops such as fruit trees even before the head-lease had been issued, revealing their confidence and their newfound feeling of land tenure security.

Besides, the CLT has facilitated the residents' systematic access to housing finance, notably through the four housing cooperatives that allowed access to funds from the National Cooperative Housing Union.

Community participation, a basis of the STDP project and the CLT's governance, should also be considered a positive impact on the community. An interesting feature of the Voi CLT lies in the fact that both landlords and tenants are involved as full members of the CLT — whereas tenants are often left out or pushed aside in upgrading projects.

Last but not least, the CLT has fostered the growth of what Midheme (2013: 80) has described as "a vibrant community premised on the principles of democracy, inclusiveness and horizontality." He went on to say that the Tanzania-Bondeni CLT has been successful in promoting:

> Solidarity — those symbiotic relations of trust, reciprocity and mutual obligation among neighbours that are so essential for community life — as a basic ingredient of the CLT. . . . In Voi, communal landholding under the CLT has offered more than just a model of land tenure; the CLT has provided the basis for residents to unite under a one-for-all, all-for-one philosophy designed to prop up each other in times of adversity.

III. THE TANZANIA–BONDENI CLT TODAY

More than twenty-five years have passed since the creation of the Tanzania-Bondeni CLT. What is the current state of the community land trust, as a neighborhood and as a community organisation?[14]

Today, the Tanzania-Bondeni settlement is a well-planned neighborhood, one that has greatly benefited from the Small Towns Development Project. The planning provisions made at the beginning of the project have been largely maintained. The physical planning undertaken in the 1990s is still visible today: the overall layout is respected and plots reserved for public utilities are respected. Although some of the plots are not yet developed and limited encroachments can be observed on areas set aside for public circulation or public utilities, a great majority of the allocated plots have been developed and the houses that were built on them are inhabited.[15]

The neighborhood still benefits from infrastructure facilities installed in the 1990s, including water, roads, and electricity. These improvements have been maintained, even upgraded. For example, the nursery school that was installed at the time of the STDP has been converted to a primary school. On the other hand, one can identify some shortcomings regarding the physical planning and regulations. The sanitation plan that was prepared at the time of the original project has not yet been implemented.

The CLT and the surrounding project have also facilitated the gradual improvement of the settlement's housing through several means. First, the local municipal government was persuaded to recognize existing dwellings on an "as-is" basis; at the same time, dwellers were required to improve their houses over a period of time to meet official building standards. Second, the CLT was accompanied by the formation of housing cooperatives, an organizational scheme that was necessary to draw public funds — especially from the National Cooperative Housing Union. As a result, the settlement has today mainly permanent structures, whereas 62% of the houses were classified as temporary structures in

Fig. 5.2. Tanzania-Bondeni. Improvement of dwellings (left) and elementary school (right).
CLAIRE SIMONNEAU

1991. A small percentage of the buildings are even multi-level dwellings.[16] However, one can still discover mud houses dispersed throughout the neighborhood, estimated at 20% of the total structures in Tanzania-Bondeni (Midheme, 2013).

A. Secured Tenure for Low-income Residents

The population in Tanzania-Bondeni is still primarily low-income. Residents use their plots and houses as their main residence and often as a place of livelihood and production as well. Importantly, absentee ownership—a threat even in a secondary town—has been avoided. As such, one can suggest that the CLT has succeeded in providing land tenure security to low-income residents over the long term.

Data from the field gathered by Midheme (2018) indicate that the average income of the majority of the population ranges from $3 to $5 per day. Additionally, 72% of the households reported that they do not own any other property outside of the settlement. The respondents who do own a property outside of the settlement are actually renters and come from outside of Voi, in other parts of the country. The survey also found out that more than 46% of the households have lived in the settlement for over 10 years.

However, the CLT has never received the head-lease for the land (only a letter of allotment) and only beacon certificates have been delivered to individual households. As a result, a lower level of legal tenure security has been ensured than would have been provided by the subleases that were initially planned.[17]

Despite that, the CLT has been effective in improving and securing land tenure for a low-income urban settlement and has restrained gentrification and mass displacement, which have happened so often in other informal settlements during the course of upgrading programmes or upon their completion.

B. Faltering Governance Structures and Unenforced Rules

The picture is less encouraging when it comes to the CLT's governance. The CLT governance mainly rests on two bodies: (1) the Tanzania-Bondeni Settlement Society, which includes all residents (tenants and structure owners) and is supposed to meet every year through an annual general meeting (AGM), and (2) a residents committee in charge of the daily affairs of the CLT, elected every two years during the AGM. Yet there has been a radical disconnection between the two bodies during the last decades, and poor implementation of the CLT's key principles.

Many key rules of the CLT are not followed anymore. In this regard, fieldwork conducted by Emmanuel Midheme, Severiano Odhiambo, Sharlet Mkabili, and Claire Simonneau in 2018 confirmed several trends that had been identified by Bassett (2005) nine years before. For example, absentee ownership is supposed to be banned within the settlement, responding to a key concern of the settlement's residents at the creation of the CLT. However, many multi-storey buildings containing rental apartments are owned by persons who are not living in Tanzania-Bondeni.

Another core commitment of the CLT model is also not being respected, namely the ban on selling land to people outside of the community. This rule is instrumental for preventing gentrification as it ensures that land is locked within the community. Residents report many land sales, however. They are called land "transfers,"[18] but a survey of residents revealed that substantial amounts of money have changed hands for these "transfers."

These violations of the CLT's founding purposes and rules are directly linked to the governance environment. First, since no sublease contractually spells out these rules, the committee has no hook to enforce them. Second, and maybe more alarming, the democratic system of the CLT seems to have collapsed.

The annual general meeting has not been held for more than 15 years. The last AGM was held in 2002, an election that had to be forced by the municipal administration. This gives a idea of the poor democratic dynamics that have characterized the community for quite a long time now. Furthermore, leaders of the residents committee (RC) are

Fig. 5.3. Tanzania-Bondeni. Multi-storey residential building. CLAIRE SIMONNEAU

perceived by the residents to be corrupt and to run the affairs of the community in their own private interest. Residents seem extremely suspicious towards their leaders, as suggested in this quotation from a resident: "Leaders are selling our lands. Leaders are selfish. Leaders are corrupt." Beacon certificates of questionable legality, signed by the RC's leaders, have been observed in the field. Also, the Tanzania-Bondeni settlement office that lies in the middle of the settlement has been deserted by the community leaders, so that there is absolutely no contact between the residents and their (so-called) representatives.

C. Community Involvement Needs to be Revived

The failure of the CLT's governance structures has contributed to a dismantling of the whole community. There are no meetings, no financial contribution to the local saving groups, a weak mobilization, and a general feeling of distrust within the community. "The CLT is good, but we have corrupt management and docile membership," says a resident. Many residents talk about the "death of the community." More than half of the residents of Tanzania-Bondeni are not members of the CLT (53%), and are not even aware of the CLT's existence.[19] They are mostly renters who settled in the neighborhood quite recently, since many owners of structures circumvent the ban on renting their houses. Thus, the CLT seems trapped in a vicious circle of land "sales" and an informal market for rental housing that fosters distrust towards leaders and fellow members of the neighborhood, even as new residents are coming into the settlement who are not aware of the CLT.

Nevertheless, there is currently a youth group that is trying to bring new life and direction to the community. This group is tracking evidence of corruption and is endeavoring to bring legal action and is pressuring to organize new elections. A local WhatsApp group has been created to foster community mobilization and to disseminate information on the mismanagement of the settlement and to discuss possible alternatives. In February 2016, the CLT office was covered with graffiti demanding elections. More recently, the youth group sent a letter to the county council and anti-corruption agency to inform them about the situation in Tanzania-Bondeni.

In sum, the Tanzania-Bondeni community and its structure of governance have been weakening over the last decade, but some recent initiatives might break the vicious circle of mismanagement and the lessening of internal cohesion and community spirit.

IV. HOW TO SUSTAIN A COMMUNITY?
LESSONS OF THE VOI CASE

The fundamental issues in Voi with regard to the current state of the Tanzania-Bondeni CLT seem to involve a lack of community spirit and a flawed structure of governance. These are challenging issues that should not be overlooked in creating a CLT.

The discussion of community organizing in Sub-Saharan Africa often revolves around the notions of ethnicity and customs — especially when it comes to land. Natural or traditional communities are based on ethnic groups and often a religious notion of the territory (such as animist or Islamic). This notion is opposed to contractual or intentional communities, which derive from discrete decisions to cooperate and to manage common resources via intentionally created institutions.

On the one hand, traditional communities based on ethnicity are still a frame of reference in politics and social relationships in Kenya and generally in Sub-Saharan Africa. Traditional landholding is based on the following principles: land is considered a sacred good, and thus is strictly unalienable and off-limits to the market logic; it is managed at a community level and people have use rights on it, not property rights. Such African traditional communal landholdings still exist, albeit with some evolution, in rural areas, and were even one source of inspiration for the first CLTs (Davis, 2010; Simonneau, 2018). Nevertheless, this framework has little relevance within the Tanzania-Bondeni community.

On the other hand, experiments with other forms of collective land holding in Kenya offer a different perspective on community building. Several legal provisions allow for collective landholding in urban Kenyan: housing cooperatives, land-buying companies, and savings-and-credit cooperatives. They are used for the sole purpose of accessing land for housing. What often happens is that the group is very active during the process of accessing the land (gathering money for buying the land jointly in the case of land buying companies for example), but as soon as the land is obtained and divided among the members, the group disbands. In other words, the organization is not an end in itself, but a means to access land in a cheaper and easier way than through formal individual landholding, which is a very long and expensive process.

Is this what happened in Voi? Probably not. The history of the Tanzania-Bondeni shows a more complex process. First, it was not based on customs or ethnicity. The Tanzania-Bondeni community was born quite naturally: people often settled there because they knew someone in the settlement. Besides, they were assigned a piece of land by a local chief. In this sense, there were *de facto* community land rules. It was a community in the full sense of the term: the settlement had been built largely through self-help; people knew each other, were aware of each other's activities and families, and had concern for each other (Bassett, 2001). The group was quite homogenous in terms of their socioeconomic situation, and there was not much ethnic heterogeneity.

Second, land insecurity made the settlement unify and become intentional at the beginning of the upgrading project. Residents realized that if they wanted to preserve the assets they already had (especially their access to land) the best method was to stay together.[20]

Third, the upgrading project fostered a modicum of community organisation and catalyzed energy in the intervening years. The project was also able to generate a large amount of positive political attention from the local to the national level and even at the international level.[21]

Nevertheless, support for the CLT was temporary. By the end of the 1990s, internal problems at the CLT had reached the ear of the local administration and had started to weaken political support for the CLT. Up until 2016, moreover, the legal and political environment in Kenya for communal landholding was clearly hostile. The recent Community Land Act theoretically offers new opportunities, but with no certainty regarding real change on the ground (Alden Wily, 2018; Bassett, 2019). This context of legal and political hostility towards communal landholding, combined with mismanagement problems, have made the CLT model less attractive for newcomers to the Tanzania-Bondeni community today.

—

V. CONCLUSION:
PROSPECTS FOR CLT DEVELOPMENT IN KENYA AND IN AFRICA

Having access to land is extremely important, since ownership builds pride and is directly connected to the sense of belonging. In Kenya and in Africa in general, the dismantling of traditional and customary institutions in the contemporary era has not eradicated the social signification of land possession. Africans still speak of being "sons of the soil."

Given the legal and political context in Kenyan, it would seem that this fundamental aspiration to participate in ownership of a piece of land is destined to be fulfilled by means of the formal or informal land market and by individual ownership. The CLT experiment in Voi has not been able to create a successful counter-example, which might serve as a compelling alternative to that of individual ownership.

From this perspective, it seems that further CLT development in Kenya and Africa would require a genuine *movement*. What is needed for a CLT movement, according to DeFilippis, Stromberg, and Williams (2018), is a strong process of community organization and empowerment. It cannot emerge if a CLT is considered solely a strategy for land access. Second, what is needed is political support that can be translated into favorable legal protections. Lastly, what has been missing in Africa is continued and targeted technical support for CLT development, which is often underestimated in upgrading projects.[22] Such support must be able to deal with the complexities of national juridical systems and also to organize national and cross-national exchanges of experience and knowledge. A substantial CLT movement might then arise in Africa and be able to influence the political economy regarding land and housing. It might then be able to exert weight in the power relations between actors of land and housing sectors, tipping the scales in a more equitable direction (DeFilippis et al., 2018).

Notes

1. We follow the definition of informal settlements elaborated by Huchzermeyer and Karam (2006: 3): "settlements of the urban poor that have developed through unauthorised occupation of land. Tenure insecurity is the central characteristic of informal settlements, with varying attributes of unhealthy and hazardous living conditions to which overcrowding, and lack of basic services may contribute."

2. Nairobi is also characterized by absentee landlords and a level of tenancy exceeding 90% (Amis, 1984; Gulyani, Bassett, and Talukdar, 2018). In other cities of the country, land squatting and a family's ownership of the building it occupies are very common.

3. An international influence that is reinforced by the presence of the headquarters of UN-Habitat (the United Nations Human Settlements Programme) in Nairobi.

4. For instance, it was selected as one of the Kenyan "Best Practices" for the 1996 UN-Habitat conference in Istanbul.

5. This essay is based on in-depth research of the Voi CLT conducted successively by Ellen Bassett and Emmanuel Midheme for their respective doctoral dissertations and by further research. Recent fieldwork was also conducted in 2018 by Emmanuel Midheme, assisted by Severiano Odhiambo and Sharlet Mkabili (Maseno University), with the participation of Claire Simonneau. For this fieldwork, we recognize and thank the financial support of the French Development Agency, which supports a research program in land-based urban commons for housing in the Global South (*https://cfuhabitat. hypotheses.org*). This work has also benefited from a fruitful exchange with the editors of the present volume.

6. Households were allocated a plot in a serviced area and were responsible for building their dwelling.

7. Even if not officially provided by the law. In Kenya in the 1990s, customary occupancy of land was quite secure since access to land was determined by the group, not necessarily by the government. Customary tenures are mostly large rural tenures. In contrast, informal settlement tenures are urban, in areas of active land markets. Customary tenure has been protected in Kenya's new constitution (2010).

8. GTZ means *Gesellschaft für Technische Zusammenarbeit,* the Agency for Technical Cooperation. GTZ is now GIZ *(Gesellschaft für Internationale Zusammenarbeit),* the Agency for International Cooperation.

9. The steps that were taken before the final vote on the land tenure option were documented by Bassett (2001: 164).

10. This was happening despite the fact that land in the Tanzania-Bondeni settlement had little market value compared to land in bigger cities.

11. Residents used two aphorisms in Swahili to express this idea: *Umoja ni nguvu* (unity is strengthen) and *Kidole kimoja hakifanyi kitu chochote* (one finger can't do anything).

12. The owners were required, however, to gradually improve their houses to conform to municipal building standards.

13. There were 818 plots, far beyond the number claimed by original structure owners.

14. This section is largely based on fieldwork conducted by Emmanuel Midheme in June 2018, and a conference given in September 2018 in Paris. Both are part of the research program on land-based commons for housing.

15. 93% according to fieldwork done in 2018.

16. 1.6% of the whole settlement; up to 8% in some specific areas (2018 fieldwork).

17. A beacon certificate is an indicator for a parcel's holder that s/he has a right to build and to stay on the parcel within the CLT. Head-leases are issued by the Ministry of Land.

18. Land transfers to relatives are allowed according to the CLT's rules.

19. Bassett (2005) previously documented this ignorance of the CLT, based on interviews dating from 1999.

20. An additional dimension relative to Voi was the age of the leadership in the RC. The Voi RC was led by older long-term residents of the community. A few of them had actually been freedom fighters. They remembered the fight for independence as a fight for land. The concept of Harambee really resonated with them; there was something of an age split on the decision, with the younger people wanting individual leaseholds. There was a high level of respect for the *wazee* (old people) in Voi.

21. The Voi Settlement Upgrading Project was selected as one of Kenya's "Best Practices" for the 1997 Istanbul Habitat II Conference. At Habitat II, the project was designated as one of the 100 best practices globally.

22. Technical support in the USA, during the early years of the American CLT movement, was provided by the Institute for Community Economics, an organization led by Chuck Matthei in 1991 when he and Russ Hahn were asked by the Ford Foundation to study whether the CLT model might be applied in Kenya.

References

Alden Wily, L. The Community Land Act in Kenya Opportunities and Challenges for Communities. *Land,* 7 (12) (2018).

Amis, P. Squatters or Tenants: The Commercialization of Unauthorized Housing in Nairobi. *World Development,* 12 (1), 87–96 (1984).

Bassett, E. M. *Institutions and Informal Settlements: The Planning Implications of the Community Land Trust Experiment in Kenya.* (Department of Urban and Regional Planning), University of Wisconsin–Madison (2001).

Bassett, E. M. Tinkering with tenure: the community land trust experiment in Voi, Kenya. *Habitat International,* 29 (3), 375–398 (2005).

Bassett, E. M. The challenge of reforming land governance in Kenya under the 2010 Constitution, *Journal of Modern African Studies,* 55 (4), 537–566 (2017).

Bassett, E. M. Reform and resistance: The political economy of land and planning reform in Kenya. *Urban Studies,* 1–20 (2019).

Bassett, E. M., and Jacobs, H. M. Community-based tenure reform in urban Africa: the community land trust experiment in Voi, Kenya. *Land Use Policy,* 14 (3), 215–229 (1997).

Davis, J. E. Origins and evolution of the community land trust in the United States. In J. E. Davis (Ed.), *The Comunity Land Trust Reader.* (Cambridge: Lincoln Institute of Land Policy, 2010).

DeFilippis, J., Stromberg, B., and Williams, O. R. W(h)ither the community in community land trusts? *Journal of urban affairs,* 40 (6), 755–769 (2018).

Durand-Lasserve, A. Le logement des pauvres dans les villes du Tiers Monde. Crise actuelle et réponses. *Revue Tiers Monde,* 29 (116), 1195–1214 (1988).

Gulyani, S., and Bassett, E. M. Retrieving the baby from the bathwater: slum upgrading in Sub-Saharan Africa. *Environment and Planning C: Government and Policy,* 25, 486–515 (2007).

Gulyani, S., Talukdar, D., and Kack, D. *Poverty, living conditions, and infrastructure access: a comparison of slums in Dakar, Johannesburg, and Nairobi.* (Washington DC: World Bank, 2010).

Huchzermeyer, M., and Karam, A. The continuing challenge of informal settlements: an introduction. In M. Huchzermeyer & A. Karam (Eds.), *Informal Settlements: a Perpetual Challenge?* (Cape Town: UCT Press, 2006).

Jaffer, M. The Tanzania-Bondeni Community Land Trust, Voi, Kenya (1996). Retrieved from *http://www.hic-gs.org/document.php?pid=2548*

Jaffer, M. Expanding equity by limiting equity. In *Property and Values: Alternatives to Public and Private Ownership* (pp. 175–188). (Washington D.C.: Island Press, 2000).

Jenkins, P., Smith, H., and Wang, Y. P. (Eds.). *Planning and Housing in a Rapidly Urbanising World* (New York: Routledge, 2007).

Kamunyori, S. W. *The Politics of Space: Negotiating Tenure Security in a Nairobi Slum*. London School of Economics (2016).

Matthei, C., and Hahn, R. *Community Land Trusts and the Delivery of Affordable Shelter to the Urban Poor in Kenya* (1991).

Midheme, E. *Modalities of Space Production within Kenya's Rapidly Transforming Cities: Cases from Voi and Kisumu*. (PhD Dissertation), KU Leuven (2015).

Midheme, E. *Do urban land commons foster urban inclusion? Kenya case study. Report on the methodological framework* (2018).

Midheme, E., and Moulaert, F. Pushing back the frontiers of property: Community land trusts and low-income housing in urban Kenya. *Land Use Policy,* 35, 73–84 (2013).

Simonneau, C. Le Community Land Trust aux États-Unis, au Kenya et en Belgique. Canaux de circulation d'un modèle alternatif et jeu d'intertextualité. *RIURBA Revue internationale d'urbanisme,* 6, (2018).

Syagga, P. Land tenure in slum upgrading projects. *Les cahiers d'Afrique de l'Est, IFRA Nairobi,* 103–113 (2011).

6.

The Origins and Evolution
of the CLT Model in South Asia

Hannah Sholder and Arif Hasan

The South Asian subcontinent has a long history of community-based landholding and community-led housing development.[1] The subcontinent also has a direct link with the evolution of the "modern" community land trust (CLT) model in the United States, given that one of its pioneers, Ralph Borsodi, was inspired by the land ownership restructuring work of India's Vinoba Bhave.[2] Bhave, who was one of Mohandas (Mahatma) Gandhi's devoted followers, spearheaded the *Bhoodan Yajna* and *Gramdan Yajna*, or land gift and village gift, movements after India gained independence from Britain in 1947.

In this chapter, the *Bhoodan* and *Gramdan* movements will be reviewed, given their historical significance for the CLT model, and their relevance as a regional precedent to current land reallocation efforts in the subcontinent. This will be followed by an overview of one of the most prominent contemporary examples of community-led development in the region, which is facilitated by the Orangi Pilot Project (OPP) in Pakistan. In the case of the OPP, while the land ownership system in which they operate does not fit the classic CLT model, their programs reflect the CLT's governance and development aspirations—led by and for the people. The OPP's programs also adapt the CLT model's housing development component, both financially and structurally, to the context of informal settlements, which is critical if the model is to flourish across the Global South.

Drawing on lessons from both the *Gramdan* movement and OPP's programs, the chapter will conclude with a look at one of the most recent efforts in the subcontinent to adapt the CLT model for tenure regularization and housing upgradation in Bangladesh's "Bihari Camps."[3] The long-term residents of these camps are seeking a permanent solution to their tenure insecurity and inhumane living conditions. They are also coming to recognize, after nearly 50 years of inaction in terms of comprehensive redevelopment by the local government and foreign donors, that no one will do this work for their benefit but themselves. Given the value of the camp lands, particularly in the increasingly overcrowded capital city of Dhaka, the residents are now facing the risk of displacement, and are thus primed to consider options such as the CLT that have the potential to protect and keep their community together.

COMMUNITY-OWNED LAND:
THE EARLY INFLUENCE OF *BHOODAN YAJNA* AND
GRAMDAN YAJNA ON THE CLT MOVEMENT

The modern CLT has its roots in the Indian *Bhoodan* and *Gramdan* movements, due in part to Ralph Borsodi's exposure to the *Gramdan* movement in India during its height in the 1960s. Starting back in the 1920s and 1930s, though, both Borsodi and Gandhi (Vinoba Bhave's predecessor) both began to experiment with alternative, community-centered lifestyles.

Borsodi and his family had left Depression-era New York City and moved to rural New York. The main impetus for their shift in lifestyle was their dislike of the increasing dependence, in urban areas, on big industry to meet one's daily needs, including shelter, clothing, and food. They opted to become "homesteaders"—building their own house and learning how to grow their own food and to make their own clothing (Borsodi, 1933; 2012). As a way to encourage others to follow suit, Ralph Borsodi founded The School of Living in 1934.

Around the same time, Mohandas Gandhi was beginning to think of such experiments as well, inspired in part by John Ruskin's *Unto This Last*, which he read while working as an attorney in South Africa. Upon his return to India in 1915, Gandhi began to carry out his visions of *Sarvodaya*, welfare of all, and *Gram Swaraj*, village self-rule, in which people would no longer be obligated to be "cogs in the machine" of industrialization. They would, instead, work together as part of self-sufficient communities. A bottleneck in the realization of *Sarvodaya* and *Gram Swaraj*, however, was that most land was owned by wealthy landowners, or *zamindars*.

In order to obtain and redistribute land for the actualization of *Sarvodaya* and *Gram Swaraj*, one of Gandhi's disciples, Vinoba Bhave, launched the land gift movement, *Bhoodan Yajna*, in 1951.[4] Coinciding with the launch of *Bhoodan Yajna*, Indian states had begun to abolish the *zamindar* land ownership system, in which wealthy individuals held large swaths of land and had many poorer individuals working their land. *Bhoodan Yajna* became one way that land was redistributed, along with new tenancy laws, registration drives, and landholding ceiling laws (Deininger, 2007).

As part of *Bhoodan Yajna*, Bhave began to travel around the Indian countryside, seeking voluntary donations of land, which were then redistributed to the landless, including former tenants of *zamindars*. However, many of these former tenant-farmers had a hard time maintaining their newly acquired land due to lack of access to credit and tools, compounded in some cases by discrimination resulting from the persistent social stigma associated with their often-times lower caste. Without larger support systems, these new small-scale farmers were vulnerable to eviction, either by physical force or by the forces of land speculation (Shepard, 2010).

Community leaders sought to address these problems through the formation of agricultural cooperatives for financial assistance, as well as through the reconfiguration of *Bhoodan Yajna* into the *Gramdan Yajna*, the village gift movement (Bhave, 1961; Shepard, 2010). The main difference between the two was that, in the village gift movement, land titles were collectively held by the Village Assembly, which was made up by all adult men and women of the village and governed by consensus. Among all the acreage contributed to the Assembly, 5% from each contributor was made available for occupancy and use by the landless; the remainder would continue to be cultivated by the original owner; but in both scenarios the actual land title would be vested in the Village Assembly. The land that was retained in use-right by the original owner was inheritable and transferable, but only within the village and only with permission of the Assembly (Dhadda, 2014).

> By 1970, over 160,000 "Trusteeships" had been established.

By 1970, over 160,000 "Trusteeships," as these communal land holdings were known in the Western world, had been established; over 4 million acres had been redistributed (Shepard, 2010). However, the movement lost traction by the mid-1970s, due to shifts in national economic policy and difficulties maintaining the Trusteeships because of a lack of funds. According to the Indian government, in 2004 only 0.7 million hectares (1.7 million acres) were still held by Village Assemblies and were largely relegated to the states of Bihar, Orissa, and Uttar Pradesh (Deininger, 2007).

Despite its decline in popularity, the *Gramdan Yajna* made a lasting impact worldwide through the growth of the CLT movement in the United States, which has now been adopted and adapted in many other regions globally. Ralph Borsodi had spent time in India tracking the land crusade of Vinoba Bhave, while on a teaching fellowship from 1961–1965. Before going to India, Borsodi had already begun to experiment with a self-sufficient lifestyle, similar to the style that Gandhi and his followers were promoting in India around the same time. But the village gift movement that Borsodi had observed in India got him thinking that what he had experimented with in rural New York could be replicated on a larger scale. In particular, he saw that land could be held in trust by the residents themselves, for the benefit of the entire community.

Inspired by *Gramdan Yajna*, Borsodi established the International Independence Institute (III) in 1967 in order to spread these new ideas of land ownership across the United States and in other parts of the world. Eventually, this organization morphed into the Institute for Community Economics and, later still, to the present-day Grounded Solutions Network, which supports CLTs across the United States. The first field director for III, Bob Swann, was directly involved in supporting the first CLT prototype, New Communities Inc., which arose in rural Georgia out of the civil rights struggle of the 1960s. In the context of the American South, civil rights leaders understood the positive impact that owning land could have on the lives of African-Americans, but they realized that:

1. Land ownership was oftentimes outside the economic reach of individuals;

2. Holding land in trust could potentially protect individuals better than private title (as experienced in the land loss that occurred in the post-Reconstruction South—similar to what happened initially with the *Bhoodan* land redistribution scheme); and

3. New landholding organizations would need the support of the wider community in order to ensure their success.

These realizations eventually gave shape to the modern CLT with its tripartite board governance system. While New Communities Inc. experienced tumultuous times as a landholding organization due to persistent discrimination, it helped give birth to a movement that continues to grow across the United States and elsewhere. Over time, as the movement spread to urban areas, the focus of many CLTs turned to the production of permanently affordable housing in addition to underpinning the ownership and stewardship of land for the common good.

COMMUNITY-LED HOUSING:
THE ORANGI PILOT PROJECT IN PAKISTAN

Back in South Asia, experiments with the production of affordable housing during the 1970s and 1980s were also taking place. One of the most prominent examples of community-led housing development emerged in Pakistan during the early 1980s. While not happening on community-owned land, the work supported by the Orangi Pilot Project (OPP) builds on the "modern" CLT's model of governance and development led by the community, with support from professionals with relevant technical expertise. It also adapts the CLT's model of housing development to the context of informal settlements, which is critical if the CLT model is to be a constructive tool for low-income households across the Global South. To this end, lessons can be taken from OPP's pragmatic model of community-financed and community-managed infrastructure upgrades, the standardization of housing repairs, and the mapping of existing tenure systems.

Background: Origins of Orangi
Township and the Orangi Pilot Project

Before the the large-scale urbanization of Karachi (with a present a population of approximately 17 million), Orangi Township, which lies in the northeastern sector of the city, was a cluster of villages inhabited by Baloch clans.[5] The area was also pasture land for their cattle and goats. Given the mass migration to Karachi following the partition of British India beginning in 1947, and other economic forces causing rural-urban migration, Karachi's population began to expand rapidly during the 1950s. In response, during the early 1960's the Karachi Resettlement Plan was put into effect, with the vision of creating two fully serviced satellite towns, including government-built housing, on Karachi's periphery for resettling migrants from India. However, the plan wasn't fully implementable due to a lack of financial and institutional capacity within the provincial government.

Given the burgeoning population's housing needs, which persisted despite the provincial government's lack of capacity, the government opted to subdivide land in peripheral townships, but not to build the housing, and only to provide the most basic services. To this end, 590 hectares (1,458 acres) of land were subdivided into small lots of 120 square meters (approximately 400 square feet), which became the core of Orangi Township. Migrant families were relocated here from inner-city informal settlements for their permanent re-settlement. The families subsequently built their own homes with the help of informal developers and contractors, while the provincial government provided them with water through truck tankers, as well as built an access road and provided transportation to the major commercial districts in Karachi.

Following Pakistan's civil war in 1971, which led to the creation of Bangladesh (formerly East Pakistan), a second immigration wave hit Karachi. Emigrants from Bangladesh, known as the "Stranded Pakistanis," resettled themselves in informal settlements which they built around the townships, including Orangi.[6] These settlements were developed by informal developers, who negotiated with officials from government land-owning agencies. A plot of land was then "sold" to the new residents, with the proceeds of the sale being divided among the land-owning department officials, the police, and the developer (Hasan, 2010).

In response to this ad-hoc development, the provincial government passed the Sindh Katchi Abadi Act in 1978 in order to regularize land tenure in these informal settlements (known locally as *katchi abadis*). While the idea of community-based collective ownership was discussed in the lead-up to the Act, what finally prevailed was a system where the provincial government maintains the ownership rights, but gives the residents of *katchi abadis* the ability to apply for a 99-year, renewable, and transferable ground lease. As this is the common practice across Karachi, residents with such a lease are able to obtain loans and can sell their houses.

With the question of urban land tenure essentially being resolved through the Sindh Katchi Abadi Act, attention became focused on improving the quality of housing and upgrading basic services and infrastructure in what had previously been informal settlements. It is with these needed improvements in mind that Dr. Akhtar Hameed Khan, a prominent South Asian social scientist, established the Orangi Pilot Project (OPP) as a nonprofit organization in 1980. Dr. Khan believed that the collapse of community-based governance systems, which had once supported community life, was causing great social and physical dislocation. In order to establish a healthy relationship between people and their government, he concluded that communities must organize once again and become directly involved in development activities. Understanding the limits of the local and provincial governments, which were under the strain of providing services to a burgeoning population with a limited tax base, Dr. Khan suggested establishing a pragmatic partnership for things like sewage system upgrades. Residents would finance and manage the sewers serving individual homes; the government would finance and manage the main trunk sewers.

This unique, pragmatic partnership took hold in Orangi Township, among other localities, increasing the political engagement of residents and improving their living conditions. In the section below the model of governance for these infrastructure upgrades will be explored, along with other innovations of OPP, including the standardization of housing upgrades, the mapping of customary tenure systems, and advocacy for the recognition of customary tenure rights in rural areas that continued to be swallowed up by urban sprawl.

Community-Financed-and-Managed Infrastructure Upgrades

When OPP began its investigation into living and social conditions in Orangi in 1980, Dr. Khan found that poor sanitation was the issue cited by residents as being the most serious problem. According to Dr. Khan, the residents knew that above-ground sewers, soak pits, and bucket latrines were causing problems not only for their health, with a significant percentage of their income being spent on medications to treat diseases spawned by unhygienic sewage systems, but also that poor sanitation reduced the value of their houses and leaseholds. Therefore, OPP conducted a survey to figure out why nothing was being done by the residents to improve their conditions if they recognized the many problems that emerged from having an inadequate sanitation system. OPP found that the major barriers to resident-led action included (Khan, 1996):

1. The belief that infrastructure development was the duty of official agencies; a charity and patronage model was also being encouraged by politicians, which led many residents to believe that an improved system would be constructed as a "free gift" before election time.

2. The conventional cost for sanitary latrines and underground sewage lines was beyond their paying capacity.

3. The residents and local masons lacked technical skills for constructing underground sewage lines.

4. Social organization for collective action was lacking in Orangi, before OPP intervened.

To address these problems, OPP initiated a Low-Cost Sanitation Program in 1981. Within three years of the program's inception, a community-government partnership had emerged, whereby the government built the external infrastructure and residents agreed to build the internal infrastructure.[7] For the management and financing of internal infrastructure, OPP staff worked with the residents to form a community organization—with a "lane," usually consisting of 20–30 households, being the primary unit of organization.

Meetings were held for each lane, during which OPP staff explained the health and economic benefits of constructing an underground sewage system and why a self-financed approach was appropriate. A lane's residents were informed that, if they elected, selected, or nominated a lane manager, then OPP would provide them with technical assistance and managerial guidance to construct and to finance a neighborhood underground sanitation system. Once OPP received a request, its technical team surveyed the lane and drew up a plan for the underground sewage system, along with estimates for the materials involved.

The plans and cost estimates were given to the lane manager, whose job it was to collect the necessary funds from each household, arrange for materials, and assist in the monitoring of the construction process. Supervision of the work was provided by the OPP technical team.[8] Sometimes two lane managers were selected by the community, with one focusing on accounting, and the other on acquiring materials and monitoring the construction process. In addition, lane managers participated in a larger federation, to handle issues such as building the intermediate sewers, which served multiple lanes (Hasan, 2010).

In addition to helping organize the lane residents for collective action, OPP offered a package of technical research, and support for replication throughout the community. As part of the research process, OPP appointed a Karachi-based architect as the principal consultant for the project. He provided advice on how to reduce costs, while increasing the quality of the products. As part of the process of implementing this advice, local masons were then trained by OPP in these new construction techniques.

For replication throughout the community, OPP gave the contact information for these newly trained masons to the lane managers so that they could be employed in the construction of the lane sewage systems. In order to facilitate the work of the lane organizations, OPP created a technical team including a professionally trained engineer and architect, and an Orangi-based plumber, draftsman and surveyor. Surveying and leveling instruments were provided to the team with financial support from a local charity and other donors. In consultation with the lane managers, the technical team surveyed the land, drafted construction documents, and drew up a list of estimated fees for labor and materials. It was then the lane manager's responsibility to call a meeting and to collect the money from each household to implement the plans in collaboration with the OPP-trained masons.

Since the program's inception, the residents have invested Rs. 138.2 million (almost $1 million USD) for internal development in 7,356 lanes (96% of households have participated). The government has invested Rs. 111.8 million in external development (OPP, 2018). Since its first iteration, the program has expanded beyond Orangi Town to 641 other urban locations in Pakistan. The 77,895 households that have participated in those locations have invested Rs. 206.2 million in internal development, and the government has invested Rs. 813.7 million.

Lessons from OPP might refine the CLT model to be applied in informal settlements across the Global South.

Due to the success of the program, in 2005 OPP's component-sharing model was made a part of the sanitation policy of the Pakistani federal government and is taught at the National Institute of Public Administration, where government officials are trained. Lessons from OPP's experience also have the potential to refine the CLT model into something that could be applied in informal settlements across the Global South. In particular, lane-based community governance and pragmatic partnership with local government could be key features to help CLTs emerge in the context of existing densely settled areas, where residents can build (or learn to build) better and cheaper for themselves, but still seek to hold the government accountable for some level of basic service provision.

Standardization of Housing Upgrades

Building on the success of OPP's sanitation program, a housing improvement program was launched in 1986. The housing program followed a similar process of research, extension, and replication. In this case, research was done to better understand the major housing issues faced by residents, with the goal of being able to offer them a package of assistance which would make construction cheaper, while improving the quality of their houses.

Research results on the major housing defects included (Khan, 1996):

1. Concrete blocks that were made manually at the *thallas* (construction yards) were substandard, brittle, and not properly compacted or cured.[9]

2. Cracked walls, on account of the weak blocks and poor masonry work, that led to excessive dampness and consequently respiratory health problems.

3. Poor ventilation, due to improper orientation of windows or mere lack of them.

4. Use of asbestos roofing materials, causing respiratory health problems and cancer, and making it difficult to build a second story (residents would have to destroy the whole structure in order to build multiple stories, since the original walls were only created to support an asbestos or tin roof).

It was also discovered that 97% of households turned to their local building component manufacturing yard (locally known as *thalla*; and the entrepreneur who operates
it known as the *thallewala*) for everything from supplies and credit to design and construction services. Given the key role these *thallas* played in the housing production process, OPP's technical advisory team determined that their initial intervention to support
housing upgrades should target the *thallas*. Thus, they started the extension process by
working with one *thalla* to upgrade its materials and production processes, endeavoring
to create better quality and cheaper materials, and to train its workers in new building
techniques. In terms of replication, OPP documented the process and invited other *thallas* to demonstrations using these newly developed materials and techniques. Within two
years, 75 *thallas* adopted OPP's recommended processes and design of materials. Today,
thallas in Orangi Township are a major exporter of quality cement blocks to the rest of
Karachi.

In 1990, OPP's technical advisory team also began to train community members to
serve as para-architects, in order to extend their package of construction advice and to
bring more community members into the housing improvement process.[10] Topics that
the *thallewallas* and the resident para-architects were trained in included (Khan, 1996):

1. How to design and build appropriate *in-situ* concrete foundations for a minimum
   ground floor plus one additional floor.

2. How to manufacture machine-made blocks, and build 6-inch-thick load-bearing walls.

3. Design advice for proper housing orientation and ventilation.

4. Molds for pre-cast concrete batten and tile roofing, as well as pre-cast staircases which
   reduced the cost by one-third.

Furthermore, in order to improve communications and to help set expectations
among the para-architects, *thallewallas* and the residents, OPP created a series of infor-
mational posters and flyers. The para-architects were also deployed, when necessary, to
monitor the work of the *thallewallas* so as to guarantee the quality of their products. This
monitoring work was done by mobile teams that visited the *thallas* as well as the houses
under construction.

Mapping and Regularization of
Customary Land Tenure Systems

As Karachi's population continued to expand and to encroach on rural village lands,
known as *goths*, OPP realized that it must also work with the original inhabitants of these
goths (who were mainly Sindhi and Baloch pastoralists) to ensure that their customary
land tenure arrangements would be recognized and honored by the government and by

private developers. During the early 2000s, many different development players were confronting these original *goth* inhabitants and claiming that, if they couldn't show any legal documentation of their land rights, then their occupancy and use of the land would no longer be recognized. Through a mix of threats, violence and pay-offs, many of the original inhabitants were evicted. OPP's campaign to halt these evictions and to restore the rights of the *goth* residents took the form of three phases:

1. mapping the *goths* and documenting their tenure arrangements;

2. forming a network of support actors, including media personnel; and

3. facilitating advocacy by the residents, including meetings with political leaders, government bureaucrats and the media.

In particular, the mapping process played a key role in the eventual recognition of the land rights of the original *goth* inhabitants, and could be a replicable and functional starting point for emerging CLTs working in informal settlements or in situations of customary landholding. In this case, OPP, through its network of support actors, was granted access to the government's existing inventory of *goth* maps, and was able to verify and to further document long-established landholding patterns. OPP then shared these augmented maps with *goth* elders, activists, government departments, and developers so that information on land ownership would be transparent.

Using these maps, *goth* leaders were empowered to take up their land tenure issues with their elected representatives, and ultimately negotiate in a more equitable manner with officials and developers. This advocacy led to the extension of the Sindh Katchi Abadi Act to the *goths*, including an extended cut-off date of December 31, 2000. This extension helped to formalize the land holding of the original *goth* inhabitants. By 2012, 1,131 *goths* were recognized through the Sindh Katchi Abadi Act (OPP, 2018).[11]

TENURE SECURITY AND UPGRADING: COMBINING FEATURES FROM CLTs AND OPP'S PROGRAMS IN BANGLADESH'S "BIHARI CAMPS"

In Bangladesh, there is a community that may be primed for the next phase of experimentation, with a potential for fruitfully combining the CLT model of land ownership with OPP's model of community-led development, in order to increase tenure security and allow for comprehensive slum upgrading in the country's "Bihari Camps." The origins of this community's tenure insecurity and current displacement risks will be discussed, followed by an analysis of their options for "rehabilitation;" that is, ways to permanently resolve tenure insecurity and improve housing conditions. Recommendations for action will also be made based on key lessons from the CLT model and OPP's programs.

Background: The Housing and Land Rights Situation
of the Camp-Dwelling Urdu-Speaking Community

After Pakistan's civil war in 1971, which led to the formation of an independent Bangladesh, hundreds of thousands of people belonging to the Urdu-speaking ethno-linguistic minority were categorically denied citizenship (in the newly formed Bangladesh) and removed from their homes. This was largely the result of the allegiance by some members

Fig.6.1. Bangladesh: roof-top view of Geneva Camp, population 25,000.

of the Urdu-speaking community to the Pakistani army during the war, who were fighting to keep the country united. Members of this linguistic minority, who also became known as "Stranded Pakistanis" or "Biharis," were to await repatriation to Pakistan in temporary internal displacement camps. However, the repatriation efforts fell short and the camps became semi-permanent.[12] At present, over 160,000 members of this linguistic-minority continue to reside in 116 camps across Bangladesh.

In 2008, after 37 years of internal displacement, a handful of the community's youth, who were born in the camps, petitioned the Bangladeshi government to reinstate their citizenship as a matter of their birthright. In an unprecedented ruling, the High Court in Dhaka affirmed their citizenship rights, which has enabled them to vote, to obtain a passport, to register for school, and to apply for jobs—albeit with persistent discrimination due to their camp address. The ruling has also impacted living conditions in the camps, although not in a positive way. It has, in fact, made the residents more vulnerable to eviction. The reason they have been allowed to stay all these years on the camp lands has been due to their status as internally displaced people. Now that they have been declared to be citizens, both the government and private owners are vying to get their land back, given that many of the camps, especially those in the capital city of Dhaka, are situated on land that has increased in value as the city's population has risen (Sholder, 2011).[13]

Options for "Rehabilitation"

In some parts of Dhaka, camp evictions have already begun, and the residents are fighting for "stay orders" from the courts until a final rehabilitation solution is determined. The camp residents are coming to realize, however, that a solution imposed from the outside may not be in their best interest, and that they must act now themselves to address their tenure insecurity. There are, conceivably, five options available to them:

1. *Return to their pre-1971 houses.* One option could be to recover the ownership and occupation rights for their pre-war housing from which they were removed. While this is the least likely option in terms of its political and logistical feasibility, it could be brought into the debate, if only as a point of leverage for the other options.

2. *Demolition and on-site redevelopment.* In 2010, the local government in Dhaka made a proposal to demolish the largest and most politically central of the camps (Geneva Camp, a population of approximately 25,000) and to house the camp's residents in 40 newly constructed, multi-storied buildings within the borders of the existing camp. Through a financial feasibility study, it was discovered that these units would be completely unaffordable for the camp's residents. In order for the project to be affordable, it would need to be heavily subsidized; given the unlikelihood of such subsidies, this plan may in reality be an instrument for the community's removal from a parcel of prime real estate (Sholder, 2014).

3. ***Demolition and off-site development.*** Another option, proposed by the local government, would be the demolition of the camps and construction of multi-storied buildings on the outskirts of Dhaka or in other localities where land is less costly. Even if the cost of land was less than in central Dhaka, the cost of construction would still need to be covered and might still result in the project not being affordable for the camp residents. In addition, removal to the hinterlands could threaten the socio-economic fabric that holds this community together—specifically living in proximity to one another and to the main commercial districts.

4. ***On-site upgrading with private title.*** Working within the existing structure of incrementally built housing, this option has enabled residents to maintain the flexibility of building as their family expands and/or as their income increases, but private titling would likely rob the camp residents of their land and improvements over the long run. The improved value, resulting from titling and upgrading, and the pull of the private market could eventually lead to gentrification. The community would likely disperse over time, as individuals "sell out."

5. ***On-site upgrading with CLT land stewardship.*** The model of community land ownership offered by a CLT may be a good option, if a camp's residents have as their primary goals to keep the community united, to secure the camp's lands for those who wish to continue to live there, and to pass on the value of their improvements to the next generation. To this end, a camp's land could be held in trust by a CLT, with its Board of Directors primarily comprised of the camp's residents. The housing on the trust land could still be privately owned and inheritable, but the CLT would have the option to set resale restrictions to ensure permanent affordability.

Recommendations and Lessons from CLTs and OPP's Programs

There are 116 camps scattered across Bangladesh. Different camps may require—and their residents may adopt—different options for a camp's rehabilitation. Not all will choose Option #5, described above, but the experiences of OPP in Pakistan and CLTs across the globe provide guidance on how residents can proceed in developing a plan of action that is right for them.

1. ***Research and consultation.*** A camp's leaders should begin by learning about the intricacies of all five options for rehabilitation. This has already begun with hundreds of camp youth attending a "community development leadership training program" from 2011–2018. Several of the trainees also attended a CLT peer exchange in Puerto Rico in 2019. A camp's leaders should then bring these options before the wider community of camp residents in order to build consensus about a way forward. The results

of these meetings would inform the organizational structure for designing and implementing an action plan.

2. *Settlement mapping.* Based on the experience of OPP, community-based mapping should be carried out to document not only who lives on a camp's lands, but also the pattern of ownership within the camp. Both pieces of information are fundamental, as they would inform any action planning to address the twin problems of tenure insecurity and the inadequacy of housing and infrastructure.

3. *Organizational governance.* Learning from the experiences of OPP, as well as from CLTs in the United States that emerged from the Civil Rights Movement, a fundamental step in moving forward would be to form an organization that not only represents and is controlled by a camp's residents, but also includes key allies. These key allies may include individuals from the majority-Bengali population, as well as experts in land law, housing development, and infrastructure upgrading. If the organization spans more than one camp, a governance structure that reflects this geography should be considered. For example, drawing on OPP's lane governance model, each camp might have its own sub-committee consisting of democratically elected managers for that camp. One or more of these managers from each camp might also serve on the larger Board of Directors of the overarching organization.

4. *Land ownership.* Once an organization is created that can speak on behalf of a camp's residents (or at least its membership) as to their united vision for rehabilitation, the organization could begin legal proceedings and/or negotiations to acquire land for the camp residents' rehabilitation. Before and after lands are acquired, a camp's residents, as represented through a newly formed CLT or some other organization, must decide how land ownership is to be structured—whether owned and stewarded by a CLT, distributed through individual land titles, or held and managed by some other arrangement.

5. *Housing and infrastructure upgrading.* If the plan for rehabilitation includes upgrading on the camp's lands, the organization should draw on financing and management lessons from OPP. In terms of finance, the Bangladeshi government may be unwilling or unable to finance upgrades in their entirety, and yet the camp residents, as newly-reinstated citizens of Bangladesh, deserve support for and access to basic services. With this in mind, OPP's pragmatic partnership with local government, splitting the cost of infrastructure upgrades, may be a reasonable approach to adopt in the context of the camps.

   In terms of management, training residents in the process of housing and infrastructure upgrades (as per OPP's experience with lane managers and para-architects) could provide key oversight. Likewise, training local construction workers in new low-cost and high-quality techniques would not only augment the local economy, but also ensure that upgrades are affordable for the camp residents, while increasing the safety and health of their homes and their neighborhoods.

—

CONCLUSION

The CLT model, adapted to the context of informal settlements, has the potential to be a useful tool for tenure regularization and upgrading across the South Asian subcontinent. The model's biggest advantages are that a CLT can keep the residents of these settlements safe from pressures and predations of the private market, and can keep the upgrading process affordable and within the community's control.

Land acquisition would be a key hurdle for CLT development in South Asia, as it is in every country. One of the main tools for acquiring rights to lands upon which informal settlements are built, especially in South Asia, could be "adverse possession" laws. While the amount of time one has to occupy the land before qualifying varies across and within countries, it may be the most financially feasible way to secure tenure by the residents of informal settlements.[14]

Despite the possibilities, one must take extreme care and caution when dealing with the issue of land rights in South Asia, and in many other parts of the world. Given that real estate is one of the most lucrative resources and industries worldwide, the process of claiming rights on land upon which there are multiple claims—whether legitimate or not—is a tricky and sometimes risky business. As a heartbreaking example of this harsh reality, it is believed that the land rights and mapping work of the late Executive Director of the Orangi Pilot Project, Perween Rahman, led to her assassination in 2013 (Ali and Zaman, 2018).

> "We are the solution, not the problem!"

With abundant caution to the real risks of this work, we must proceed forward on the path of justice and equity. With this in mind, our Bangladeshi colleagues are launching their campaign to address the long-outstanding issue of the "rehabilitation" of the camp-dwelling Urdu-speaking community in Bangladesh. They are also investigating the possibility of utilizing the CLT model of land ownership and governance along with Bangladesh's adverse possession law to claim rights to lands within the "Bihari Camps." They are holding meetings to build support and consensus on a path forward, and will then propose their plan to the government. As leaders from several of these camps discovered, when attending a peer exchange with leaders of the Caño Martín Peña CLT in Puerto Rico, "We are the solution, not the problem!"

Notes

1. Prior to the Mughal period of rule in the South Asian subcontinent (1526–1857), during which the *Zamindar* system of private land ownership grew, most land was considered the aggregate wealth of a community and collectively managed (Bandyopadhyay, 1993).

2. The modern CLT is based on the ownership of land for the common good, instead of "ownership in common." The land is held by a nonprofit organization that is typically governed by a tripartite board, with two-thirds of the members being from the identified service area (one-third residing on the CLT's land and one-third living in the surrounding neighborhood); the remaining third is made up of technical experts, representatives of other NGOs, and (sometimes) representatives of government.

3. The "Bihari Camps" are internal displacement camps in Bangladesh that have been in existence since Pakistan's 1971 civil war, which led to the formation of an independent Bangladesh (formerly East Pakistan). To this day, 160,000 people still reside in 116 camps.

4. An acute land conflict in the South Indian village of Pochampalli is what instigated the *Bhoodan* movement. In this village, two-thirds of the residents were landless and had been seeking support from the government, but to no avail. The landless residents sought guidance from Bhave while he was passing through on his quest to implement *Sarvodaya* and *Gram Swaraj*. Bhave called a meeting to see if this conflict could be resolved without intervention from outside forces. Perhaps being influenced by Bhave's vision for the future, one of the village's wealthy landlords offered 100 acres of his own land to be redistributed among the landless residents (Mehta, 2001).

5. The Baloch are an ethnic group living predominantly in the Sindh and Balochistan provinces of Pakistan.

6. Approximately 25% of Orangi's inhabitants today are "Stranded Pakistanis," now also referred to as "Biharis," who came from the internal displacement camps in Bangladesh following Pakistan's 1971 civil war.

7. The external infrastructure consists of trunk sewers, long intermediate sewers, and treatment plants. The internal infrastructure consists of a latrine in the house, a one-chamber septic tank connecting the latrine to the lane sewer (to prevent solids from entering the sewers), the sewer in the lane, and the intermediate sewer, when not too long.

8. At no point did OPP touch the money of the lane organizations or determine how it was to be spent, or interfere in the election of the lane managers.

9. Manual block-bearing load = 100 pounds per square inch (psi) versus a mechanized block-bearing load = 800–1000 psi.

10. In 1999, two community members who were trained as para-architects also founded the Technical Training Resource Center, providing design advice, complete with drawings and estimates, to Orangi residents. The Center also helps to build social infrastructure such as schools and clinics (Hasan, 2010).

11. Building off the success of OPP's mapping program, its sanitation and housing programs along with a savings and loan program were extended to the *goths*. Although, shortly after these programs were initiated in the *goths*, they were scaled back due to the assassination of OPP's Executive Director, Perween Rahman (which is discussed in this chapter's conclusion).

12. Some of those who were interned in the Bihari Camps eventually made it to Pakistan and resettled on the outskirts of Orangi Town in Karachi. Of those who settled in Orangi Town, some have become the beneficiaries of OPP's outreach; thus, providing a direct connection between these now geographically-distinct communities, which could ultimately facilitate the extension of advice.

13. Some of the Bihari Camps were built on vacant parcels of privately and publically owned land. Other camps take the form of former schools and market halls, as well as abandoned houses, which were used as temporary housing following the 1971 war. However, these lands and buildings were never returned to their original uses. Plans by the government, international donors or community members themselves were never made for their "rehabilitation."

14. Adverse possession may apply in Bangladesh after 12 years of occupation if the rightful owner does not bring eviction proceedings within this period (Red Cross, 2017). In India, the timeframe is separated for private and public lands, with 12 years and 30 years being the respective occupation thresholds (Law Commission of India).

References

Ali, N.S. and Zaman, F. (2018). "Perween Rahman's murder: the great cover up." *Dawn.* *https://www.dawn.com/news/1319812/perween-rahmans-murder-the-great-cover-up*

Bandyopadhyay, R. (1993). "Land Systems in India: A Historical Review." *Economic and Political Weekly* 28 (52):149–155.

Borsodi, R. (2012). *Homesteading: Flight from the City. An Experiment in Creative Living on the Land.* Reprint of 1933 edition. Middletown: CreateSpace Independent Publishing Platform.

Bhave, V. (1961). "The Path of Love." Pp. 186–205 in M. Brown (ed.), *The Nationalist Movement: Indian Political Thought from Ranade to Bhave.* Berkeley: University of California Press.

Deininger, K., Jin, S., Nagarajan, H. (2007). "Land Reforms, Poverty Reduction, and Economic Growth: Evidence from India." Washington DC: The World Bank.

Dhadda, S. (2014). "Vinoba Bhave's Gramdan Movement." Satyagraha Foundation for Nonviolent Studies. *http://www.satyagrahafoundtion.org/vinoba-bhaves-gramdan-movement/*

Hasan, A. (2010). *Participatory Development.* Karachi: Oxford University Press.

Khan, A.H. (1996). *Orangi Pilot Project: Reminiscences and Reflections.* Karachi: Oxford University Press.

Law Commission of India. (n.d.). "Consultation Paper-cum-Questionnaire on Adverse Possession of Land/Immovable Property." *http://lawcommissionofindia.nic.in/reports/Adverse%20Possession.pdf*

Mehta, S. (2001). "Bhoodan-Gramdan Movement—50 Years: A Review". Mumbai: Gandhi Book Center. *http://www.mkgandhi-sarvodaya.org/bhoodan.htm*

Orangi Pilot Project. (2018). Quarterly Report. *http://www.opp.org.pk/opp-rti/*

Red Cross (2017—draft). "Housing, Land and Property Law in Bangladesh." *ShelterCluster.* *https://www.sheltercluster.org/sites/default/files/docs/bangladesh_hlp.pdf*

Shepard, M. (2010). "Gandhi Today: A Report on Mahatma Gandhi's Successors." Pp. 108–112 in J.E. Davis (ed.), *The Community Land Trust Reader.* Cambridge: The Lincoln Institute for Land Policy.

Sholder, H. (2011). "Housing and Land Rights: The Camp-Dwelling Urdu-Speaking Community in Bangladesh." Dhaka: Refugee and Migratory Movements Research Unit.

Sholder, H. (2014). "Physical Rehabilitation and Social Integration: The Camp-Dwelling Urdu-Speaking Community in Bangladesh." Berkeley: UC Berkeley Department of City and Regional Planning.

7.

Challenges for the New Kid on the Block—Collective Property

Liz Alden Wily

A study was published in July 2018 by the World Resources Institute, examining the quest of private companies to secure formal title to land, compared to communities looking to do the same (Notes et al., 2018). Companies found titling to be easy and fast, while communities struggled with complex and costly procedures. This was hardly surprising given the heated climate of globalized demand for land in which "ease of doing business" has become a benchmark. More interesting was that the driving question was no longer "is it possible for communities to register as owners?" The study simply presumed the answer to be "yes."

This reflects changing times for the nearly three billion land dependents who acquire and hold lands through customary, neo-customary, or more recently, state-established community-based tenure systems. At six to seven billion hectares, the global community's land area is half or more of the world's lands (LandMark, 2019). Less than one-fifth of this is formally registered, and public maps of these lands cover less than fifteen percent (15 percent) of these. Nevertheless, it is now possible for communities in *most* countries to secure lands as their formal property, as indicated in state-compiled land registers. While a great deal is involved in reaching the point of registration for communities, this possibility contrasts starkly with the situation 50 years past.

In fact, the strength of legal change affecting collective landholding suggests that this may feature prominently in the land registers of the world by the end of the current century. By hectares, community property may eventually account for the largest sector of state-recognized landholdings.

If this is so, it will be no mean achievement in context of the (very) long *dureé*, considering that Aristotle and Plato feistily debated the relative merits of individual and communal tenure two-and-a-half millennia ago (Pipes, 1999). The matter was put to bed by Rome a millennium later (509 BC–AD 395) as the city state expanded into an empire, turning thousands of captured hectares into *ager publicus* (public land) for disposal by the Emperor to (privileged) individuals. The next millennium saw these Roman norms profoundly shape European property law and, thence, the statutory laws of effectively all 195 modern states today. The odd exception aside (Mexico in the 1930s stands out), it has only been during the last half century that states have come to recognize communally held lands as something more than permissive occupation on unowned or government lands.

> Collective lands are, at one and the same time, material property and an inseparable regime of community-based land governance.

Before this new development is explored, questions arise. First, *what exactly is the identity of this exciting and perhaps excitable new kid on the property block?* Depending on the country and framework, collective property is termed communal, collective, customary, native, indigenous, or community land. These properties are variously vested directly in the community or held in trust for them by a cooperative, shareholding, or non-shareholding and nonprofit body like a community land trust, the subject of the present volume.

The most common feature across the species is that the landholding has a socio-spatial basis involving residents who have an identifiable social identity as communities or groups. These are not corporations comprising remote or disparate individuals, acting for disparate shareholders unknown to each other. It is also usual for the social group to hold lawful decision-making rights. Collective lands are, at one and the same time, material property and an inseparable regime of community-based land governance.

A second question might be: as land is a finite resource, with little of it beyond the polar regions that is deemed unowned today, *where is this supposed cornucopia of collective holdings coming from?*

The answer is that these collective holdings derive almost entirely from *ager publicus,* which modern governments define as their own property under government, state, national, public or similar categories. Thousands of rural communities live therein, their traditional right-holding arrangements overlaid by such classifications, reducing them in law to tenants at will. This has made them easy to evict for greater ambitions of the state, including the plethora of large-scale allocations to foreign and local investors. It is the belated transformation of ownerless occupancy into legally protected property interests that principally anchors contemporary tenure reforms. And, as elaborated later, it is anxiety by governments around the consequent decline in the scale of the state-controlled *ager publicus* that poses the greatest constraint to the delivery of acknowledged community property, beyond legal declamations that this exists or can be entrenched through formalization.

A third question is: *Why would modern communities prefer to secure lands collectively rather than through individual entitlement?* To generalize, settled farming communities in particular *do* seek private rights to well-established house plots and farms within community domains. However, while permanent farmland will expand from its present 11–15 percent of global land area (FAO, 2015), the larger resource of most communities is comprised of naturally collective forests, rangelands, swamps, steep areas, and arid lands. These landscapes are neither easily nor productively divisible into individual parcels and, where shifting cultivation is practiced, not all areas are distinct from farms. The importance of shared off-farm land resources to livelihood and socio-culture is such that communities are loathe to lose them.

The habit of Twentieth Century farm titling programmes of co-opting all but permanent farms as government property has also left a legacy which communities do not want to see extended in de facto compulsory individualization, where this remains the only means to gain state recognition of rights. Communities are equally wary of losing the accessible, adaptable, and cost-free decision-making and dispute resolution that governs community-based tenure. Millions of rural communities have seen these powers transferred to remote government offices, not easy or free to access or to hold to account (Bruce *et al.*, 2013). State trusteeship of customary lands has been a particularly ripe arrangement for abuse. Sustaining the right to *govern* local landholding has become a core element of community land claims today.

> Sustaining the right to govern local landholding has become a core element of community land claims today.

The same concerns can be found among communities in fertile zones whose domains are almost entirely comprised of family properties, such as in Fiji, Gabon, or family lands across the Caribbean. Even without substantial collective assets to protect, community jurisdiction over rural lands continues to provide social assurance of rights, continuity in social norms (such as around land inheritance), protection from elite land-capturing interests, and solidarity for decision-making where single voices against external threats do not prevail. These concerns are echoed in urban areas, as noted in other essays in the present volume, examining community land trusts.

This helps to answer a fourth pair of questions: *Is collective property only relevant to the rural domain, and is not the rural domain declining with urbanization?*

To address the second of the pair first, this presumption needs modification. While cities and towns indisputably dominate in terms of population, they absorb surprisingly little land, from one to three percent globally, not expected to exceed eight to ten percent by the century's end (Mertes *et al.*, 2015). It is true that rural population growth is not expected to keep growing, other than in Africa and Asia where absolute numbers will rise (UN, 2018). A high proportion of community lands are in these regions. In

> There exists a massively
> untapped potential for the
> adoption of collective property
> norms in urban areas.

addition, rural communities already face soaring demand for a share of their lands by urban dwellers with origins in those villages (Jayne *et al.* 2016). Classical distinctions between rural and urban domains is becoming more, not less, blurred in agrarian economies, supporting findings that many urban dwellers want to see home rural communities and their lands survive. And while, ideally, farms will expand and intensify to help feed 11 billion people by 2100, even if this has tripled by that year, the major land resource will remain neither urban nor farmed, but exist in billions of hectares which are by character naturally communal — forests, pastures, waterlands, mountains, etc. Not surprisingly, communities are their logical guardians. As failures in resource conservation rise and threats of climate change mount, the formal empowerment of communities as forest and rangeland owners has risen as an advocated strategy, with most implementation thus far in the natural forest sector (RRI, 2018).

Meantime, there exists a massively untapped potential for the adoption of collective property norms in urban areas, especially in city slums where 2.5 billion will live by 2050, the majority of them in Asia and Africa. This is because the poorest live in fragile shelters on parcels too small to render individual titling a practical path for regularization of occupancy. These are also areas where community (neighborhood) governance evolves as a matter of necessity to provide services and to protect human rights. Even when slum dwellers have the opportunity to convert compressed shacks into a high-rise apartment block, inclusion requires cooperation and solidarity. It is partly in light of this urban potential that it was suggested earlier that collective tenure, despite roadblocks, could become the major form of property in time.

How realistic is this? This is a hard call, because another reality is that a legal framework for collective property may widely exist on paper, but is complex to achieve in practice. The rest of this essay looks at what exists in law, and the constraints confronting this reform.

LEGAL PROVISION FOR COLLECTIVE PROPERTY

A global comparison of 100 national land laws in 2018 found that 73 of these laws provide for communities to secure lands as collective owners (Alden Wily, 2018). In addition, two-thirds stipulate that collective properties enjoy legal force and effect on a par with registered individual and corporate properties.

Such provisions have historically been most prevalent in Latin America and Oceania and, more recently, in Africa. They are least available in the Middle East. In Europe, some countries have never extinguished communal landholding (e.g. Switzerland, Austria, Ireland, Norway, Sweden) and there has been a recent revival in countries like Spain and

Portugal, as the logical route to protect fire-threatened forests and pastures. There has also been resuscitation of suppressed community ownership of forests and pastures in some former Soviet Union states and satellites, since the Soviet Union's collapse in 1989. Examples are Romania, where communities now lawfully own and govern 800 communal forests and pastures, and Armenia, where the most local level of state cooperatives that existed under Soviet rule have been converted into some 400 community-owned and administered areas.

Types of socially-collective property vary. At one extreme are modern state-defined collectives, such as provided in one million rural communities in China, which together cover 49 percent of China, albeit with community control that is sometimes frustrated by the number of Communist Party directives. At the other extreme are parliaments which have seen to fit to simply declare, either in national constitutions or land laws, that customarily held lands are now deemed to be property, whether owned by individuals, families, or communities, thus covering all types of estates. This is now the case in around fifteen African countries, from Kenya to Mozambique to Liberia. Other laws are less fulsome in the support they provide, such as not fully liberating communities from root title held by chiefs or governments; or they fail to provide easy and cheap routes through which communities can double-lock their rights in entitlements. In between these extremes are tenures like the community land trust, where lands are held by a community-controlled NGO, which acquires, holds, and manages real property on behalf of a place-based community.

Thousands of communities are already titled owners. Examples include: the case of China above; indigenous communities in Australia and Canada, who respectively hold title to 30 and 44 percent of the acreage in those countries; 32,000 indigenous and farming communities, who own 52 percent of Mexico; 7,200 indigenous and farming communities in Peru; and an estimated 20 percent of the Philippines that is subject to Certificates of Ancestral Title of Domain. There are other examples, including Fiji, Vanuatu, Papua New Guinea, Tanzania, Mozambique, Malawi, Mali, and Uganda, where titling is not compulsory. On paper, customary ownership is unaffected, although case-by-case titling is underway. Arrangements differ. In Tanzania, 12,450 elected village councils legally govern tenure within their recorded domains. Although individual and family rights may be recorded in village land registers and certificates of title issued, the community must first record the shared lands to protect these from encroachment.

While many other cases of legally secure community-based tenures exist, the majority of community lands globally are not yet acknowledged and secured as property, nor have these lands been designated exclusively for community-based tenure and governance (RRI, 2015).

The 2018 study of national land laws found a significant difference between the 44 percent of countries in the study's sample that acknowledge community property as already

> Legal provision for community property has been slowly rising.

existing and protect these rights in principle, and the 55 percent of national laws that guarantee recognition and protection only where community property is formally adjudicated, surveyed, and registered. This opens the door for reluctant governmental administrations to delay titling.

Requirements to establish legal entities in which to vest title have also handicapped delivery of title to community property in several countries, including Peru and Australia. The Ivory Coast is notorious in this regard, where the titling procedure has proved so expensive and bureaucratic that not a single community has been successful since 1998. The law was amended in 2013 to ease this.

Legal provision for community property, however, has been slowly rising since 1980, especially since 2000 (49 percent of first-time legal provision). At least two new laws have been enacted since the study was published in mid-2018 (Liberia and Tunisia). At least ten more countries currently have bills in parliament (e.g. South Africa) or in circulated draft (e.g. Ghana), or under draft (e.g. Nepal, Myanmar, Sierra Leone, Indonesia). Demand remains high. Coverage is also expanding from indigenous peoples to populations of all types, recently including former slave communities in parts of Latin America. In fact, two-thirds of the laws examined by the World Resources Institute in 2018 did not specify the populations to which these laws applied. This trend is represented at the international level in the UN's *Declaration on the Rights of Peasants and Other People Working in Rural Areas* (2018), designed to cover all rural communities and requires, *inter alia*, individual and collective land rights to be upheld.

Legal content is also maturing. The newest laws strongly require inclusive decision-making within communities, including provisions for enabling members who have moved to cities for education or for work to be permitted to vote on matters specified as most important. Added to some of these laws is a requirement that lands be zoned or re-zoned to ensure that communal areas are not randomly encroached upon. Stipulations are also appearing requiring communities to record parcels under accepted exclusive family or individual usufruct, defined as inheritable and disposable interests in accordance with community rules.

These measures lessen the pressure to privatize all lands for the purpose of securing rights. Nevertheless, the desire to secure houses and farms as absolutely private property is quite likely to remain, ultimately subtracting such settlements from the overall community domain, focusing collective tenure on shared lands.

Meanwhile, it is more common today for new laws to define a place-based community as a juridical person, alleviating any need for the formation of a corporate entity in which to vest title. Some define community in such a manner that an urban community could adopt the same construct, which is already the case in Vietnam, Laos and China. Newest enactments, where some or all of the above are apparent, include countries as far apart as East Timor, Kenya, Liberia, Malawi, Mali, Vietnam, Tunisia and Vanuatu.

THE LIMITS OF LEGAL PROVISION

Of course, what the law says and how it is applied are different matters. Push-back can begin early, as in countries where governments fail to enact essential application decrees or regulations, even a decade after a law is enacted (e.g. Argentina and Angola). Quite a number of governments have taken years to budget for supporting institutional and survey services. Even where laws for titling community property have been enacted and applied, some governments have eventually found a reason to turn back the clock, enacting inhibiting regulations (e.g. Peru), halting new allocations (e.g. Brazil), or even doing away with the relevant law altogether (e.g., Antigua and Barbuda). Court rulings can also take their toll. In India, for example, the Supreme Court in February 2019 ordered that forest peoples be evicted in 21 states, potentially affecting 8 million of the poorest land-dependents, despite being guaranteed ownership under a Forest Rights Act of 2006. On appeal, a "stay" of the eviction was temporarily granted, returning the case to the Supreme Court.

> Orthodoxies die hard, including beliefs that collective landholding is archaic.

More subtle means of curtailing collective land rights occur through natural resource and investment laws, through which watersheds, traditionally-mined surface minerals, sites of cultural importance, and even public service areas which communities themselves have instituted on their lands, are redefined by the government as public, not community property. Declaration of investment zones and infrastructural corridors have the same effect. Public interest is often expanded to cover commercial investments and investment zones. Security zones requiring the eviction of all inhabitants also occurs. Another tactic being deployed is the accelerated official declaration ("gazettement") of state-owned protected areas. This removes yet more forest, wildlife-rich rangelands and waterlands from communities, all essential to local economies. In short, push-back from governments has been substantial.

Reasons for this are quite similar across regions. Orthodoxies die hard, including beliefs that collective landholding is archaic; that wealth creation and capital surplus for investment can only be triggered through individual or corporate accumulation; and that land markets only work with individual, fungible rights. The fact that communist regimes in the Twentieth Century co-opted and reconstructed collective tenure as state-owned production units also undermined the case for community-based collective property as a viable basis for economic growth. Insufficient progress has yet been made in demonstrating the contrary; namely, that growth and development can be achieved through strategic investment in community-owned land and co-owned investor-community enterprises, in which a place-based community is the lessor.

Instead, orthodoxies are being revitalized by the fast globalizing land market, feeding commercial and government capture of large lands in what has commonly been referred to as a "global land rush." A decade after the 2008 financial crisis, this land rush is no longer a temporary surge, but a fixture in bilateral trade relations. Untitled community lands are an obvious and easy target, encouraging governments to "adjust" the definitions of public, government, and community lands. Thousands of communities have been involuntarily displaced by their governments to make way for such land-based investments and their supporting infrastructure.

Compulsory land acquisition laws are not being reformed as quickly as needed to make assistance for resettlement obligatory, nor to compensate takings at levels that come anywhere near to replacement costs. Governments are hardly proactive on these matters with the notable exception of India, due to landmark legislation in 2013. Laws in other countries may even limit rather than expand the grounds on which compensation is required in cases of compulsory acquisition and may value communal lands at levels far below their livelihood and social values.

Yet the greater source of governmental reluctance to move forward swiftly to help communities to double-lock their land domains in formal titles stems from a belated recognition by governments that, by acknowledging community ownership in the first instance, they risk depriving themselves of millions of hectares that a government has come to assume as their own, under a previous designation as public or government lands. The increasing value of natural resources adds grist to governmental reluctance to reduce the public estate. This is the case from Afghanistan to Brazil, from Uganda to Cambodia, and from Timor Leste to Madagascar.

Yet, once out of the box, Pandora, in the form of accumulating recognition of millions of rights under the aegis of community tenure, is not easily returned to its suppressed condition. Modern communities are increasingly well-versed in constitutional rights. They communicate among themselves. They are loath to surrender strengthening paths to land security. They are more demanding of international support. Recourse to the courts is becoming common on all continents, although hardly swift or necessarily incorruptible. Protests against land takings are on the rise, sometimes with fatal results for the land defenders. It seems inevitable that this thread of social transformation will continue, but not without difficulty. In truth, brave optimism aside, it is still too early to predict where the balance will lie half-a-century hence.

Bibliography

Alden Wily, Liz, "Collective Land Ownership in the 21st Century: Overview of Global Trends, *Land,* 7, 68 (2018).

Bruce, John, Tidiane Ngaido, Robin Nielsen, and Kelsey Jones-Casey, *Land Administration to Nurture Development (Land), Protection of Pastoralists' Land Rights: Lessons from International Experience,* USAID (2013).

FAO (UN Food and Agriculture Organization) "World Agriculture: Towards 2015–2030: A FAO Perspective", FAO (2015).

Jayne, Tom, Jordan Chamberlain, Lulama Traub, Nicholas Sitko, Milu Muyanga, Felix Yeboah, Ward Anseeuw, Antony Chapoto, "Africa's changing farm size distribution patterns: the rise of medium-scale farms," *Agricultural Economics* 47 (2016): 197–214.

LandMark, Global Platform of Indigenous and Community Lands (www.landmarkmap.org).

Mertes, C., M. Schneider, D. Sulla-Menashe, A. Tatem, B. Tan "Detecting change in urban areas at continental scales with MODIS data," *Remote Sensing of Environment* 158 (2015): 331–347.

Notes, Laura, Peter Veit, Iliana Monterroso, Andiko, Emmanuel Sulle, Anne Larson, Anne-Sophie Gindroz, Julia Quaedvlieg, Andrew Williams, World Resources Institute (WRI), *The Scramble for Land Rights Reducing Inequity between Communities and Companies* (Washington: World Resources Institute, 2018).

Pipes, Richard, *Property and Freedom* (New York: Alfred A. Knopf, 1999).

Rights and Resources, Woods Hole Research Center, LandMark, "Towards a Global Baseline of Carbon Storage in Collective Lands, An Updated Analysis of Indigenous Peoples' and Local Communities' Contribution to Climate Change Mitigation" (2016).

Rights and Resources Initiative (RRI), *Who Owns the World's Land? Global baseline of formally recognized indigenous & community land rights* (Washington: RRI, 2015).

Rights and Resources Initiative (RRI), *At a Crossroads Consequential Trends in Recognition of Community-Based Forest Tenure from 2002–2017* (Washington: RRI 2018).

United Nations, *World Urbanization Prospects: The 2018 Revision.* (New York: UN Economic and Social Affairs 2018).

ABOUT THE CONTRIBUTORS

Liz Alden Wily, PhD (Political Science), is a specialist in land tenure, working as a researcher, technical adviser, and practitioner on community landholding. She has worked on this issue in approximately twenty countries. Liz has been instrumental in helping to launch regional and global initiatives in support of community land rights such as LandMark, an online facility which collates maps and information about community lands. She is a Fellow at the Leiden Law School's Van Vollenhoven Institute, a Fellow at Katiba Institute, a constitutional advocacy body in Africa, and a Fellow of the Rights and Resources Initiative, a global coalition.

Line Algoed is a PhD researcher at Cosmopolis, Center for Urban Research at the Vrije Universiteit in Brussels and a Research Fellow at the International Institute of Social Studies in The Hague. She works with the Caño Martín Peña CLT in Puerto Rico on international exchanges among communities involved in land struggles. She is also an Associate at the Center for CLT Innovation. Previously, Line was a World Habitat Awards Program Manager at BSHF (now World Habitat). She holds an MA in Cultural Anthropology from the University of Leiden and an MA in Sociology from the London School of Economics.

Patricia Basile is currently a visiting scholar at the Latin American and Iberian Institute of the University of New Mexico. Her change-oriented research aims to support the pursuit of equity and power for those who have been historically oppressed, especially in the Global South. Basile holds a PhD in the Constructed Environment from the University of Virginia, a Professional Masters in Building and Urban Sustainability from the Mackenzie Presbyterian University, and a Bachelor of Architecture and Urban Planning from the same university. Before moving to the United States, Patricia worked on several social housing and favela upgrading projects in São Paulo.

Ellen M. Bassett is a Professor in Urban and Environmental Planning at the University of Virginia and Chair of the department. She worked from 1989 to 2001 as a technical advisor with bilateral aid agencies and international NGOs in Kenya and Uganda.

Her current research is focused on land rights and planning law reform in Kenya. Among other publications, she is the author of *Institutions and Informal Settlements: The Planning Implications of the Community Land Trust Experiment in Kenya* (2001). She holds a PhD, MS, and MA from the University of Wisconsin-Madison.

ALEJANDRO COTTÉ MORALES holds a PhD in Social Policy from the Graduate School of Social Work of the University of Puerto Rico, Río Piedras Campus, where he is an Adjunct Professor. He has 25 years of experience as a community social worker. From 1994 to 2002, he directed the Community Development Area of the Península de Cantera Project. In 2002, he became Director of Citizen Participation and Social Development for ENLACE and the Caño Martín Peña CLT. He was instrumental in guiding grassroots organizing and participation processes around those initiatives, as well as advising on comprehensive development.

MARÍA E. HERNÁNDEZ-TORRALES holds an LLM in environmental law from the Vermont Law School and an MA in Business Education from New York University. She studied for her undergraduate and Juris Doctor degrees at the University of Puerto Rico. Since 2005 she has been doing pro bono legal work for the Proyecto ENLACE and for the Fideicomiso de la Tierra del Caño Martín Peña. Since 2008, Hernández-Torrales has worked as an attorney and clinical professor at the University of Puerto Rico School of Law where she teaches the Community Economic Development Clinic.

MEAGAN M. EHLENZ is an assistant professor at Arizona State University's School of Geography and Urban Planning. Her major fields of study include urban revitalization and community development, with specializations in shared equity homeownership models and anchor institution strategies in urban places. Ehlenz holds a PhD in City and Regional Planning from the University of Pennsylvania and a Professional Masters in Urban Planning from the University of Wisconsin-Milwaukee. Prior to pursuing her PhD, Ehlenz was a planning practitioner with experience as a private-sector planning consultant and a public-sector senior planner for the City of Milwaukee's Department of City Development. Ehlenz is a certified planner with the American Institute of Certified Planners.

JOHN EMMEUS DAVIS is a founding partner of Burlington Associates in Community Development, a national consulting cooperative. He was housing director in Burlington, Vermont under Mayors Bernie Sanders and Peter Clavelle. Community land trusts have been a prominent part of his professional practice and scholarly writing for nearly 40 years. His publications include *Contested Ground* (1991), *The Affordable City* (1994), *The City-CLT Partnership* (2008), *The Community Land Trust Reader* (2010), and *Manuel* *d'antispéculation immobilière* (2014). He co-produced the film, *Arc of Justice,* and is president of the Center for CLT Innovation (*https://cltweb.org*). He holds an MS and PhD from Cornell University.

TARCYLA FIDALGO RIBEIRO is Co-coordinator of the Favela CLT program at Catalytic Communities in Rio de Janeiro and a researcher for the Metropolis Observatory, a project led by Rio de Janeiro's Federal University which encourages reflection about cities and urban planning in Brazil. She holds a Bachelor's Degree in Law and a Master's Degree in Urban Law from the State University of Rio de Janeiro. She has done post-graduate work in urban sociology and in urban planning and policy at the Federal University of Rio de Janeiro, where she is presently enrolled as a doctoral candidate.

ARIF HASAN is a Pakistani architect, planner, activist, teacher, and researcher who has taught at universities in Pakistan and Europe and served on several UN committees dealing with urban issues. He is the author of numerous books, research papers, and monographs on poverty, planning, and development. He was the Principal Consultant and, later, the Chairperson of the Orangi Pilot Project-Research and Training Institute (1981–2017). He is the founding Chairperson of the Urban Resource Centre Karachi, a founding member of the Asian Coalition for Housing Rights, and a member of the boards of multiple international academic journals and research organisations.

EMMANUEL MIDHEME teaches at the School of Planning and Architecture, Maseno University, Kenya. He earned his PhD in Spatial Planning and Urban Development from the University of Leuven, Belgium in 2015. Emmanuel's current research focuses on the role of land tenure and property in the production of equitable and inclusive spaces in rapidly transforming cities of sub-Saharan Africa. He is interested in how marginalized urban groups employ everyday practices of commoning and social innovation to meet needs unsatisfied by conventional market and state mechanisms. Emmanuel has previously researched and published on the Tanzania-Bondeni Community Land Trust, Africa's first CLT.

LYVIA RODRÍGUEZ DEL VALLE is the former Executive Director of the Caño Martín Peña CLT and Corporación Proyecto ENLACE del Caño Martín Peña. For over 15 years, she worked with an interdisciplinary team and community organizations on implementation of the ENLACE Project. Lyvia previously worked on urban revitalization in San Juan and risk management and decentralization in Quito and Asunción. She holds a master's degree in Urban and Regional Planning and a graduate certificate in Latin American Studies from the University of Florida, Gainesville, and a bachelor's degree in Environmental Design from the School of Architecture, University of Puerto Rico.

HANNAH SHOLDER is a housing, community, and economic development specialist who has worked with a formerly displaced community in Bangladesh since 2009, supporting efforts to improve their housing and land rights situation. Also in Bangladesh, she co-founded a minority youth leadership summit in 2011 and a women's handicraft cooperative in 2014. In the Washington D.C. area, where she currently resides, Ms. Sholder serves as Director of Land Stewardship for a nonprofit that creates, preserves, and manages urban farms for the purpose of hands-on agricultural education. She is a Fulbright Scholar with two MAs from the University of California, Berkeley.

CLAIRE SIMONNEAU is a geographer and an urban planner. She is currently a researcher at CNRS, the national scientific research center in France, coordinating a research program on land-based commons for housing in the Global South. She holds a PhD in urban planning from the University of Montreal, Canada. Her research interests relate to land issues, urban management and governance in the Global South, and the field of "urban commons." She has also had substantial professional experience working with development aid organizations in West Africa.

KARLA TORRES SUEIRO (ktorressueiro@gmail.com) is a lawyer specializing in socioeconomic and citizenship rights. She is a Staff Attorney at the ABA Pro Bono Asylum Representation Project, providing legal representation for unaccompanied children in immigration detention at the south Texas border. Karla previously assisted with appeal cases from EU citizens in the UK who were exercising their rights of citizenship and residency. She joined the Caño CLT in 2016, where she helped to manage the worldwide exchange of knowledge about forms of collective land tenure. She holds an LLM in International Criminal Justice and Human Rights from the University of Kent.

KIRBY WHITE worked for the Institute for Community Economics in the 1980s and 1990s, writing and editing technical materials for CLTs, including *The Community Land Trust Handbook* and the first two editions of the *Community Land Trust Legal Manual*. He was a co-editor of ICE's journal *Community Economics* (1983–1996) and provided direct technical assistance to CLTs in urban and rural communities throughout the United States. Later, he was employed by Equity Trust, Inc., developing technical materials for agricultural land trusts, including the 2009 publication, *Preserving Farms for Farmers*. He has also written several novels dealing with environmental and community development subjects.

NOLA WHITE is a founder and the current president of the Honduras Community Support Corporation (*http://www.hcsc-honduras.org*). She also helped to organize FECOVESO (*Fundación Eco Verde Sostenible*), a regional land trust and community development organization based in Honduras. Previously, Nola supervised Bennington

College's "Field Work Term" program; worked as a tenant organizer, fighting to save an "expiring use" rental housing project; coordinated a local food cooperative; and provided transportation and support for immigrant farmworkers. In the 1980s, she served on the board of the Institute for Community Economics and was a member of ICE's loan committee, evaluating loan applications from CLTs.

THERESA WILLIAMSON, PhD, is a city planner and founding executive director of Catalytic Communities, an NGO working to support Rio de Janeiro's favelas through asset-based community development. CatComm produces *RioOnWatch,* an award-winning local-to-global favela news platform, and recently launched Rio's Sustainable Favela Network and a Favela Community Land Trust program. Theresa is an advocate for the recognition of the favelas' heritage status and their residents' right to be treated as equal citizens. She received the 2018 American Society of Rio prize for her contributions to the city and the 2012 NAHRO Award for her contributions to the international housing debate.

www.ingramcontent.com/pod-product-compliance
Lightning Source LLC
Chambersburg PA
CBHW080558030426
42336CB00019B/3233